EST Marathon '95
The Complete One-Act Plays

EST Marathon '95
The Complete One-Act Plays

Edited by Marisa Smith
Introduction by Curt Dempster

Contemporary Playwrights Series

SK
A Smith and Kraus Book

A Smith and Kraus Book
Published by Smith and Kraus, Inc.
One Main Street, PO Box 127, Lyme, NH 03768

Manufactured in the United States of America

Cover and Text Design by Julia Hill

First Edition: October 1995
10 9 8 7 6 5 4 3 2 1

Library of Congress Cataloguing-in-Publication Data

EST Marathon '95 : the complete one-act plays / edited by Marisa Smith ; foreword by Curt Dempster. --1st ed.
p. cm. -- (Contemporary playwrights series)
ISBN 1-880399-85-7
1. One-act plays, American. 2. American drama--20th century. 3. Ensemble Studio Theatre.
I. Smith, Marisa. II. Ensemble Studio Theatre. III. Series.
PS627.053E882   1992
812'.04108--dc20   95-39321
CIP

Dedication

To Heléne and Stephen Gordon
for their long-term support and true philanthropy
which has sustained The Ensemble Studio Theatre's
yearly Marathon Festival of One-Act Plays.

Contents

Introduction

It is a rare pleasure to be writing an introduction to Smith and Kraus's *second* volume of one-acts from The Ensemble Studio Theatre. The first highly successful book of plays from the '94 Marathon of One-Acts was a very seminal event for us and all the writers involved. It opened new possibilities for one-act productions and brought strong original pieces to new readers across the country.

This year's edition of plays features a newly rediscovered one-act by our undervalued American genius Thornton Wilder, and we were very proud to produce this unique piece and to have it reach print along with the other World Premières by veteran, emerging, and new writers.

Producing one-acts is a way to prove commitment to writers. It expedites growth, provides freedom from the "home-run" syndrome of success and allows a writer great latitude in exploring form and content. It is our hope at E.S.T. that this volume and its predecessor will send a beam of energy across our land to producers, directors and actors. If you want to contribute to the artistic life of the American Theatre, produce one-acts at your regional theatre, college, or community theatre. In doing so, you will be giving precious opportunities to deserving writers and providing your audiences with a new variety of theatrical enjoyment. And it's a great way to develop new talent.

On behalf of all our members in New York and California and our extraordinary Board of Directors...

Curt Dempster, Artistic Director, Ensemble Studio Theatre

Flyboy
by Yvonne Adrian

BIOGRAPHY

Yvonne Adrian is the 1994 recipient of the New York Foundation for the Arts Artists' Fellowship Award given for Playwrighting. *Flyboy* was developed with Director Maggie Mancinelli-Cahill at The Ensemble Studio Theatre, with Artistic Director, Curt Dempster. *Flyboy* was also presented by Playwrights' Preview Productions Urban Stages Series; Artistic Director, Frances Hill. Ms. Adrian's full-length play, *Legendary Siren,* developed at EST in the *In Pursuit of America* project is optioned by CPC Productions, California as a screenplay. Her works in the EST Annual Octoberfests include *Dive! Faxyou!, Black Tights & Leotard, Colors, Unlikely Companions, Hail to the Queen, Cooky's Four Tunes.* Her new full-length musical, *Vanity and Vexation,* was presented in workshop by the Obie winner, theatre company, The New Group; Artistic Director, Scott Elliott. Her short play, *Fountainbleu-di-Fellini* was produced in the *Water Plays* at Alice's Fourth Floor; Artistic Director, Susann Brinkley. Her current work-in-progress, *Hollywood Blonde,* a one-woman show was presented at Alice's in *May Plays.* Ms. Adrian is a member of The Dramatist's Guild, Inc. ASCAP, The Ensemble Studio Theatre, The New Group and Alice's Fourth Floor.

AUTHOR'S NOTE

Flyboy is dedicated to my son, Matthew Puckett, a fine young man and musician. His story became the inspiration for this play. Therefore I wrote *Flyboy* solely, from the point of view of the child, as he envisions the adult world. The first draft of *Flyboy* was written with the character of Zachary, heard only as drumbeats offstage. In the second draft, he became a real boy. In the final draft, musical underscoring was added to augment the words/music. The actors do not have to be singers. I worked with jazz musician Bruno Destrez. Musical tapes are available and can be used by permission of Mr. Destrez by contacting the author.

I chose a nonlinear form, stylistic in nature and surrealistic in tone as it allowed me to travel the characters through time and distance without restrictions.

Special thanks to Roger Puckett, Tim Cahill, Lourdes Garcia, Ross Charap, Polly Adams, Jennie Ventriss, Miranda Kent, Ilene Kristen, Bob Fisher, T.L. Reilly, Leigh Armor, Abraham Burton, Playwright's

Preview Productions and all casts involved in the development of *Flyboy.*

After a long and arduous search, my husband and I finally discovered The Churchill School for Special Education in Manhattan. My heartfelt thanks to Mr. Harry Valentine and the staff of teachers, especially Ms. Kristy Baxter and Ms. Naomi Gutheil.

ORIGINAL PRODUCTION

Flyboy was first produced in The Ensemble Studio Theatre 1995 One-Act Play Marathon. It was directed by Maggie Mancinelli-Cahill (stage manager, William Tivenan; musical director, Richard Mover; music by Bruno Destrez) with the following cast:

Mom	Christine Farrell
Zachary	Adam Fox
Dr. Pontiff	Salty Loeb
Teacher	Ellen Mareneck
Dr. Neurosian	Richard Mover
Dad	Dan Ziskie

CHARACTERS

MOM: 35–45, Busy. Anxious.

DAD: 35–45, Busy. Anxious

ZACHARY: Eight years old. Unable to read and unable to get a word in edgewise, he stops talking and yearns to fly his own music. Can be played by an older boy. Actor does not have to play drums.

TEACHER: Female. Aggravated.

DR. PONTIFF: Female. Befuddled.

DR. NEUROSIAN: Male. Precariously precise.

CHILDREN/CHORUS: Are played by Dr. Pontiff and Dr. Neurosian.

TIME

Today

SETTING

USA

NOTE

The storyline of *Flyboy* concerns five adults caught up in a child's world and is told solely through the point of view of Zachary. Although the play is not children's theatre, it is stylized and should be approached engagingly in the spirit of the colorfully illustrated storybooks of children—à la Maurice Sendak. The set requires the use of one table, center and four chairs or cubes. A prop of one balloon is used to indicate the glass apple. Scenes between the parents and son are to be played with heightened reality. Scenes between the parents, doctors, teacher, and Zachary, are surrealistic. As directed at E.S.T. the character of Dr. Neurosian played the drumbeats for Zachary. All actors remain on stage at all times. Actors do not have to be singers.

FLYBOY

PROLOGUE

Theatre in the Black. Music interlude. Prologue. Lights up, music out. Scene: Z's bedroom.

ZACHARY: *(Motor sounds.)* Errrrrrrrrr!Errrrrrrrrr! *(Zachary enters. He runs. Arms outstretched, he holds drumsticks, like the wings of an airplane. Flies. Spirals up and down. Goes into a spin. Comes in for the landing.)* Pilot to copilot! Prepare for landing! *(Brakes screech to a halt.)* Eeeeeeeeeeeeeeeeeeee!

MOM: *(Calls. Offstage.)* Zeeeeeeeeeeeeeeeeee! What's all the racket?

ZACHARY: Oh…*(Grabs his shirt.)*

MOM: *(Enters.)* Why aren't you dressed?

ZACHARY: I'm trying to get dressed…*(Struggles.)*

DAD: *(Calls.)* C'mon! Gotta go!

MOM: *(Takes drumsticks.)* Give me the drumsticks.

ZACHARY: Wait Mom!

MOM: Now!

ZACHARY: *(Reluctant.)* Mom!

MOM: *(Puts drumsticks away.)* Your shirt's on backwards.

ZACHARY: Whattayamean my shirt's on backwards…

MOM: Let me fix it. *(Fixes.)* Tie your shoes. *Loop*-it! *Loop*-it! The other way!

ZACHARY: Mom!

MOM: I said the *other* way. *(Fixes.)*

ZACHARY: OW!

MOM: Let me fix it!

DAD: *(Calls.)* Time to eat!

MOM: The drumsticks are going into the closet.

ZACHARY: But!

MOM: To stay! Let's go.

DAD: *(Calls.)* Breakfast! *(He enters.)*

    (All rush to table. Mom/Dad blow kisses.)

DAD: How are you, Z?

ZACHARY: I'm…

DAD: *(Shoves toast into Z's mouth.)* Here's your toast.

MOM: *(Argues.)* He likes cereal.

DAD: *(Argues.)* He likes toast.

MOM: Cereal.

DAD: Toast.

MOM: Cereal!

DAD: Toast!

    (Drumbeats in. During following dialogue as argument builds. Z. beats the air to drown out Mom/Dad.)

MOM: I'll fix it.

DAD: I fixed it.

MOM: Cereal?

DAD: Toast!

MOM: Cereal!

DAD: Toast!

MOM: CEREAL!

DAD: TOAST!

    (Drumbeats increase in tempo.)

MOM: Z!

DAD: Z!

MOM: Z!

DAD: Why does he *do* that?

MOM: *(Indicates.)* Here's your books.

DAD: *(Hands Z. a balloon.)* A glass apple for the teacher.

MOM: Very hard to find.

DAD: Very fragile.

MOM: Be careful!

DAD: Watch the books.

MOM: Don't lose 'em!

DAD: Don't scratch 'em!

MOM: Keep 'em nice!

DAD: Bring 'em home!

MOM: They're special.

DAD: You're special.

MOM: Very very special.

    (Drumbeats in as Z. runs backwards.)

DAD: But he *walks* backwards.

    (End of Prologue. Light change.)

SCENE ONE

Urgent phone ring. Brrring! Brrring!

TEACHER: *(With frustration.)* This is Zachary's teacher. Your son stopped talking at school today.

MOM: Stopped talking?

TEACHER: He does not talk. He will not talk. He refuses to ATTEMPT to talk.

MOM: Refuses?

TEACHER: Yes!

MOM: No!

TEACHER: Talk to him.

DAD: *(Goes to Mom.)* What's wrong?

MOM: She says he won't talk.

DAD: What're you talkin' about?

MOM: She says he just stopped.

DAD: Why?!

MOM: What's going on in his head?

DAD: *(Calls.)* Z!

MOM: Honey.

DAD: Son.

ZACHARY: *(No response.)*

DAD: How are you?

ZACHARY: *(No response.)*

MOM: Do you have a sore throat?

ZACHARY: *(No response.)*

DAD: Earache?

ZACHARY: *(No response.)*

MOM: Toothache?

ZACHARY: *(No response.)*

DAD: If you don't talk you can't go to school.

MOM: You'll have to stay home!

DAD: You won't learn.

MOM: You'll be bored.

DAD: Wattaya have to say?

ZACHARY: *(No response.)*

DAD: No more games!

ZACHARY: *(No response.)*

DAD: *(Takes Z aside.)* I'll take care of this. C'mon now, between you and me, what's goin' on? *(Silence.)* It's the women, right? *(Silence.)* Your mother talks too much, right? *(Silence.)* Your teacher, right? *(Silence.)* You can tell me, okay? *(Silence.)* Okay? *(Silence.)* Okay! You're grounded for *life.*

(Light change. Urgent phone rings. Brrring. Brrring.)

TEACHER: *(Clinched teeth.)* Your son does not read. He will not read. He refuses to attempt to read. Come in and see me this afternoon.

SCENE TWO
Third Degree

Mom/Dad go to teacher. Zachary goes to Mom

TEACHER: *(More frustrated.)* Do you know your son has not one ounce of attention span?

MOM: No.

TEACHER: Do you know your son is a jokester?

DAD: No.

TEACHER: He jumps around. Scribbles gibberish on the blackboard.

MOM: Gibberish?

TEACHER: He clowns like Charlie Chaplin!

DAD: Clowns?

TEACHER: Encourages the other children to clownaround.

MOM: Ohdear…

TEACHER: Are you aware he does not respect authority?

DAD: No.

TEACHER: In class he takes his pencil. He BEATS *(Beats her pencil.)* on everything.

MOM: Beats…?

TEACHER: Do you read to him?

MOM: Of course I do.

TEACHER: What do you read?

(Music in. Word/Music: MOM'S FRACTURED NURSERY RHYME.)

MOM: *(To Zachary.)* We read *Cat In The Hat,*
Green Eggs And Ham,
Sam I am!
Or is it, I am Sam?
Jacob Two Two,
(spells.) T!W!O!
Wee Manny, Big Coo,
Where'd Penelope go?
Amelia Bedlia,
Mister Bump!
Dr. Seuss,
Some book about mumps!
Shel Silverstein,
Light In The Attic!
(Music Out.) So, what's all the fuss? His mind is not static.

TEACHER: I've only seen his POP-UP books.

MOM: Pop-Up books? Are you implying?…

TEACHER: At Pop-Up books! He only looks!

DAD: So what if it pops! What're you trying? You got a good book. Give it to 'im. Let him hold it, let him look. He'll read it. Who cares if it's Tin-Tin, Superman or the funny pages?

(Music in. Jazz riffs underscore Teacher's dialogue. Word/Music: TEACHER'S LAMENT.)

TEACHER: He does not know a P from a B. Or a B from a D. Nor an E from an F, or a J from a G, or a G from a J! If a J can be G, then a G is a C. Put it together, he thinks it's a THREE! I teach too many kids. He won't learn from ME. He's sent into the hall. Outside the class. Working-alone-on-his-own. MAYBE he'll pass.

(Music out.)

MOM: *(Turns to Dad.)* Why can't he read?

DAD: Reading takes time.

MOM: I was a fast reader.

DAD: I was slow, so!

MOM: What should we do?

DAD: We'll try making magic.

MOM: Magic?

DAD: Magic with Flash Cards.

MOM: *(Physically enacts.)* Z. You can do it! Start with A!

DAD: Apple.

MOM: B!

DAD: Baby.

MOM: C!

DAD: Cat.

MOM: D!

DAD: *(Music in.)* Dammit, son.

   (Light change. Indicates heightened reality, as Zachary envisions the following.)

MOM: *(Gibberish.)* Blah-lah-A!-gumba-B!-eht-ton-C!-a-ton-flom-blom-yah-D-schru-mah-A!-ton-dah-B!ton-dah-C!-na-ton-H!goom-bah-D!-a-roA!-a-ton-B!-nah-brow-C!-glob-blah-D!-tay-mah-A!
   (Word/Music: CACOPHONY.)

MOM: *(Staccato.)* A.B.C.D.

TEACHER: *(Demand.)* Take your seat and stop crying.

DAD: Just do it.

CHILDREN: Tee hee, Tee hee, Tee hee.

TEACHER: Keep your eyes on the page. Until you know the word.

MOM: A.B.C.D.

TEACHER: Say it outloud!

MOM: A.B.C.D.

DAD: Just do it.

CHILDREN: Tee hee, Tee hee, Tee hee.

TEACHER: Keep your eyes on the page.

MOM: A.B.C.D.

TEACHER: The.

MOM: A.B.C.D.

DAD: Just do it.

CHILDREN: Tee hee, Tee hee, Tee hee.

TEACHER: Keep your eyes on the page! The!

MOM: A.B.C.D.

DAD: Just do it.

CHILDREN: THE. THE. THE.

TEACHER: Say it out loud.

CHILDREN: THE. THE. THE

MOM: A.B.C.D.

TEACHER: Keep your eyes on the page!

CHILDREN: THE. THE. THE

DAD: Why the hell can't he *do* it?

TEACHER: On the page! On the page!

ALL/TEACHER: On the page, on the page, on the page! *(Repeats.)* Page! The! On! The! On! Page! Page! Page! *(Repeats. Then mouths in silence as...)*

(Music out. Lights change. Flurry of drumbeats.)

ZACHARY: *(Beats the air.)*

DAD: He's beating on his books!

MOM: That's no way to treat books!

DAD: He's destroying his books!

MOM: You have to stop him.

DAD: Why is it always me?

MOM: I said stop him!

DAD: Z! Z! Your mother said to stop!

(Music in. Zachary stops.)

SCENE THREE
Zachary's Flight #1

Zachary's theme filters stage. Z. flies into his world. Until...Lights change. Urgent phone rings. Brring. Brring

TEACHER: Zachary jumped off the school stoop today. Cracked his teeth on his knees. He's at Mt. Sinai. I suggest you see the shrink. *(Siren.)*

SCENE FOUR
Taxi #1

Music in. Mom/Dad enter taxi. Bounce in backseat.

DAD: *(To driver.)* Mt. Sinai!
MOM: Tell the driver to go faster.
DAD: The Teacher prob'ly shoved him.
MOM: Tell the driver to change lanes.
DAD: Teethmarks on his knees.
MOM: Tell the driver we're stuck!
DAD: Kneebones in his teeth.
MOM: Let's get the subway.
DAD: I'm not having a heart attack.
MOM: It's the light that's stuck!
DAD: I'll get a checkup.
MOM: How many more blocks?
DAD: I'll be fine.
MOM: Are we there yet?
DAD: He'll be fine.
MOM: *(Yells at driver.)* Take another street!
   (Music out. Sound of honk.)

SCENE FIVE
Mt. Sinai #1

Mom/Dad go to Dr. Pontiff. Dialogue overlaps.

DAD: Dr. Pontiff?
DR. PONTIFF: Uh, yup? Uh yup?
DAD: Has he said anything?
DR. PONTIFF: Ohyeah, well, uh, how could he?
MOM: Are we the problem?
DR. PONTIFF: Uh, Well uh, lemme see.
DAD: Could it be?…
MOM: *(Finishes Dad's sentence.)* He was born three weeks late?

DR. PONTIFF: I dunno, could be.

DAD: He never slept well.

MOM: Cried a lot.

DR. PONTIFF: Yeah, well, uh, maybe so, could be.

DAD: Could be WHAT?

DR. PONTIFF: Yeah, well, could be that too.

DAD: What do we do?

DR. PONTIFF: Uh, uh, uh, well, uh, relaaax.

DAD: But he's losing his hair!

DR. PONTIFF: *(Checks Zachary's hair.)* Oh, uh, yup, yup.

DAD: I found a small round bald spot.

MOM: *(Finishes Dad's sentence.)* The size of a dime on his head.

DR. PONTIFF: Uh, well uh. Where?

DAD: There! Could it be from worry?

DR. PONTIFF: *(Winces.)* Could be. Yeah, could be.

MOM: Could it be alopecia?

DAD: Is it fatal?

DR. PONTIFF: I dunno, maybe.

DAD: It *is* fatal??

MOM: *(Reads quickly.)* Look, it says right here. Alopecia means area baldness. Loss of hair varies from partial to total!

DAD: *(To Dr. Pontiff.)* Why a sudden bald patch?

DR. PONTIFF: Sudden bald patches occur from uh, uh, some reason or other.

DAD: Shouldn't it be dealt with?

MOM: Is it psychological?

DR. PONTIFF: Oh. Oh. Oh. Uh, Hmmm, well, you know. Hmm. *(To Zachary.)* Are your looks important?

MOM: It says right here, sometimes it happens all over the body!

DR. PONTIFF: Uh yup, uh-huh, Yup, yup. That's what it says.

DAD: Can he be cured?

MOM: Does it have to do…with not talking?

DAD: Everything's stuck in his head?

DR. PONTIFF: Maybe, maybe so.

DAD: Tell us what to do!

DR. PONTIFF: Uh well, uh, you could uh, why don't you, uh, uh, uh, try to relaaax!

MOM: This is too much stress!

DR. PONTIFF: Well uh, maybe uh, could be that!

DAD: I never hit him!

MOM: I never raise my voice!

DAD: I never tease him!

MOM: I never say no!

DAD: Why doesn't he like me?

MOM: Why isn't he like other kids?

DR. PONTIFF: *(To Dad.)* Do you *play* with him?

DAD: Play?

DR. PONTIFF: *(To Mom.)* Do you spend *time* with him?

MOM: Time?

DR. PONTIFF: Oh, yup, yup, and oh, oh, it's that time. Uh well uh, Sorry, it's that *time.* Uh hmm uh hmm, uh hmm, uh hmmm.

SCENE SIX
Playtime

Mom/Dad take Zachary's hands.

DAD: *(Pulls Zachary.)* Let's play.

MOM: *(Pulls Zachary.)* You're on my time.

DAD: What'll we play?

MOM: *(Tug of war.)* It's my time.

DAD: *(Tug of war.)* My dear, it's playtime.

MOM: My dear, it's my time.

DAD: Playtime.

MOM: My time.

DAD: Playtime.

MOM: My time!

DAD: Playtime!

MOM: Your time's tomorrow.

DAD: Today at four!

MOM: You had a meeting.

DAD: I canceled the meeting.

MOM: I came home early.

DAD: Not early e-nuf!

    (Drumbeats in. Zachary beats the air.)

MOM: Earlier than you.

DAD: Quality time's with me!

MOM: Me.

DAD: Me.

MOM: Me!

DAD: Me!

> *(Drumbeats increase. Mom/Dad mouth "Me" dialogue in silence. Music in. Light Change.)*

SCENE SEVEN
Zachary's Flight #2

> *Zachary flies. Arms outstretched. Until...Music out. Phone rings. Brring. Brring.*

TEACHER: *(Aggravated.)* Zachary tried to slide down the slide today. Standing right straight up with his arms flying. He's at Mt. Sinai! *(Siren.)*

SCENE EIGHT
Taxi #2

> *Music in. Mom/Dad enter taxi. Bounce in backseat.*

MOM: *(To driver.)* Mt. Sinai!

DAD: I could hit him.

MOM: Who taught him to crawl?

DAD: I could choke him.

MOM: Who taught him to stand?

DAD: I could drown him.

MOM: Who taught him to walk?

DAD: I could bite him.

MOM: Who taught him to run?

DAD: I could tease him.

MOM: Who bought him skates?

DAD: I could dislike him.

MOM: Who bought him skiis?

DAD: He said, "Daddy, please!"

MOM: What about the toy bus? The toy train, the toy jeep, the toy plane?

DAD: *(Yells at driver.)* Take another street!
  (Music out. Sound of honk!.)

SCENE NINE
Mt. Sinai #2

Dr. Neurosian peers into Zachary's eyes.

DOCTOR NEUROSIAN: *(Expounds.)* He does NOT see red. He does NOT see green. Quite frankly, he does not know where the sidewalk ends. I tested him for brain damage.

DR. PONTIFF: Ah-Haah!

DAD: Is he retarded?

MOM: Is it a concussion?

DOCTOR NEUROSIAN: He does not perceive of himself or others within the framework of his own circumference.

DR. PONTIFF: Could be.

MOM: Is he autistic?

DAD: Is he dyslexic?'

DOCTOR NEUROSIAN: He must know where the sidewalk ends. Meanwhile, he must take these little half-pink, half-blue PILLS.

MOM: Drugs?

TEACHER: Sometimes pills should take pills.

DR. PONTIFF: Could be.

DOCTOR NEUROSIAN: Half-pink allows him to focus. Half-blue changes his personality. Then he'll talk. Fill the prescription!

DAD: Prescription for what?

DOCTOR NEUROSIAN: Hyperkinetic Ritalin-istic Syndrome.

DR. PONTIFF: Could be that too.

MOM: Is it eye to hand?

TEACHER: Uh.

DAD: Inner ear?

DOCTOR NEUROSIAN: Uh.

MOM: I've read certain sounds disturb kids.

DR. PONTIFF: Uh.

MOM: Does he speak through his music?

DR. PONTIFF: Sounds good.

DOCTOR NEUROSIAN: *(Non-stop.)* It points to a deficiency of cells of the left brain which handles fast sounds. The medial geniculate nucleus of the thalamus, processes impulses on the way to the auditory cortex which then interprets speech which then...

DAD: *(Interrupt.)* What the hell does that mean?

DOCTOR NEUROSIAN: Fill the prescription!

TEACHER: I would say it's what he's fed! Food's the toxic potion. Seems as tho, it affects his head, comes out...

DOCTOR NEUROSIAN: Perpetual motion.

TEACHER: Perpetual motion.

DAD/MOM: *(In unison.)* Perpetual motion?

> *(Music in. Word/Music: PERPETUAL MOTION. Teacher, Doctor Neurosian, Doctor Pontiff.)*

TEACHER: Sugar will DO it.

ALL: Perpetual motion,

TEACHER: He never will sit,

ALL: Perpetual motion,

TEACHER: CANdy's a culprit,

ALL: Perpetual motion,

TEACHER: You better COMMIT,

ALL: Perpetual motion!

> *(Zachary joins rhythms.)*

NEUROSIAN: JUNK food, JUNK food,

ALL: Perpetual motion,

NEUROSIAN: Affects your MOOD,

ALL: Perpetual motion,

NEUROSIAN: Soft drink *So*-DAH'S!

ALL: Perpetual motion,

NEUROSIAN: Make you a LOAD-AH!

ALL: Perpetual motion!

NEUROSIAN: Eliminate SWEETS now...

TEACHER: Eliminate SWEETS now...

NEUROSIAN: Or he'll run amuck.

TEACHER: Or he'll run amuck.

PONTIFF: Uh-muck, uh-muck, uh-muck, uh-muck.

NEUROSIAN: That's ten thousand bucks,

DAD/MOM: Ten thousand bucks?

NEUROSIAN/PONTIFF/TEACHER: Ten thousand bucks,

ALL & DAD/MOM: That's ten thousand bucks.

PONTIFF: Uh-Huh! Uh-Huh! Uh-Huh!

NEUROSIAN: Hear us, MOMMY, POPPY,

TEACHER: No CHOC-CO-LATE! or cheese,

NEUROSIAN: Kids get HOPPY WOPPY,

ALL: Now pay our fees, please!
   Wooo! Wooo! Wooo! Wooo!
   Wooo! Wooo! Wooo! Wooo!

DAD/MOM: For TEN THOUSAND BUCKS?

ALL: Ten thousand bucks!
   Perpetual motion, perpetual motion,
   Perpetual motion, perpetual motion
   (Carried away.) Perpetual motion!
   (Music out.)

DOCTOR NEUROSIAN: *(Spoken.)* Fill the prescription!

DAD: *(To Zachary.)* I'm going broke Z. Can't you do anything right?!
   (Zachary turns to Dad. Tears wellup. Lights change.)

SCENE TEN
X-Pell

   Phone rings. Brring. Brring.

TEACHER: Yes. I *X*-pelled him!

DAD: *X*-pelled? How could you?

TEACHER: He FLEW off my desk. Without warning. I sent him home.

DAD: Home? You should have called us first!

TEACHER: He devastated my classroom!

DAD: Why?

TEACHER: I don't know WHY. I was out of the room.

DAD: Why were you out of the room?

TEACHER: I was gone for a moment. When I returned he FLEW. He broke my glass apple.

DAD: *(To Zachary.)* How? When? Where? What? Why??

(Lights change. Zachary envisions the following. Word/Music: DRAW THE LINE.)

TEACHER: Draw the line.

ZACHARY: *(Bounces balloon.)*

TEACHER: From closet to clothes. Shoes to feet. Pillow to bed.
Draw the line.
(Music in.)

TEACHER: *(Clinched teeth.)* Closet-to-clothes. Shoes-to-feet. Pillow-to-bed.
Draw the line.

CHORUS: Closet to clothes. Shoes to feet. Pillow to bed.
Draw the line.

TEACHER: That's not it. Try again.
Tire to car, Lid to jar, Comb to head.
Draw the line.

CHORUS: Tire to car, Lid to jar, Comb to head.
Draw the line.

TEACHER: That's not it. Try again.
Tire to car, Lid to jar, Comb to head.
Draw the line.

CHORUS: Tire to car, Lid to jar, Comb to head.
Draw the line.

TEACHER: That's not it. Try again.
Tears to cheeks, Tissue to nose, Nozzle to hose.
Draw the line.

CHORUS: That's not it. Try again
Tears to cheeks, Tissue to nose, Nozzle to hose.

TEACHER: That's not it. Try again. That's not it. Try again.

TEACHER/CHORUS: Draw the line. Draw the line. Draw the line!
Draw the line. Draw the line. Draw the line. Draw the line!
(Balloon pops. Music out.)

TEACHER: You broke my glass apple. You broke my GLASS APPLE.)

SCENE ELEVEN
In the Closet

MOM: How could she send him home all by himself?

DAD: Where is he?

MOM: I can't find him.

DAD: Z!

MOM: Why is it so quiet?

DAD: Did you try the closet?

MOM: The closet?

DAD: Try the closet!

MOM: Honey…?

DAD: Is he there?

MOM: Oh God…

DAD: What?

MOM: He made a sculpture of sheets…

DAD: All white…

MOM: How'd he drape all that material…?

DAD: Do you see him?

MOM: Do you?

DAD: There.

MOM: What if he's…?

DAD: Is he…?

MOM: Z?

DAD: Z?

(*Mom goes to Z. Holds him in her arms.*)

MOM: *(Relief.)* Scared me to death!

DAD: *(Relief.)* Damnit!

MOM: *(Temper.)* I never liked that teacher!

DAD: *(Temper.)* I will not have my kid hiding in the back of a closet!

DAD AND MOM: *(In unison.)* NO MORE X-PERTS!

MOM: You're his father. What do we do now?

DAD: You're his mother. What do you think?

MOM: I think it comes from your side of the family.

DAD: My side? Your side!

MOM: No, your side! My side are the talkers.

DAD: Your brother never writes.

MOM: Your sister never calls.

DAD: Your mother!…

MOM: *(Overlaps.)* Your father!

DAD: What about my father?

MOM: *(No response.)*

DAD: *(Loses it.)* You're telling me I don't know how to be a father?
   (Flurry of drumbeats.)

MOM: *(Obviously not.)* I'm sorry.

DAD: No, I'm sorry.

MOM: No, I'm sorry.

DAD: I'm sorry!

MOM: I'm sorry!

DAD: No, I'm sorry!
   (Music in. Word/Music: LULLABY TO Z.)

MOM: *(To Zachary.)* Dear one…

DAD: *(To Zachary.)* Had no father in my childhood,
   Can I soothe you anyway,
   Son, can I be any good,
   Not knowing what to do or say?

MOM: Sweet one…

DAD: When you were a baby boy,
   Carried you wrapped in my arms,
   Ev'n at two and three and four,
   Protected you from worldly harms.

MOM: Small one…

DAD: Easy to say, Be A Father,
   Must know how. 'Tho I am lost,
   Had I known my one…no bother,
   Dad's for you, at any cost.
   (Music out.)

MOM: Father, Father, up in heaven,
   Guide us, help us hold our hand,

DAD: I'll abide to guide my son, sir.

DAD/MOM: *(In unison.)* Send the word.
   (Lengthy pause. Mom/Dad listen for an answer from above. They wait. No response.)

DAD: What's the matter with us?

MOM: Where've we been?

DAD: *(To Z.)* Son, you're the only one that counts. *(Picks up drumsticks. Hands them to Z.)*

ZACHARY: *(One beat.)*
DAD/MOM: What, Z?
ZACHARY: *(Flurry.)*
DAD/MOM: Okay! *(Correct.)* ZACHARY!
ZACHARY: *(Goes wild on drums. Wild with antics.)*
DAD: Heyhey, stop! I said stop! You're driving me crazy.
MOM: Waitaminute! He's acting just like us!
ZACHARY: *(Wild flurries.)*
MOM: What's that?
DAD: Oh, we're driving *you* crazy!
ZACHARY: *(One beat.)*
MOM: So, you have to get away.
DAD: That's why you fly to your music.
ZACHARY: *(One beat.)*
DAD: Can't tell us from where…
ZACHARY: *(One beat.)*
MOM: It's just there…
DAD: Can we go there with you?
MOM: Up in the air?
DAD: Is it safe?
ZACHARY: *(Flurry.)*
DAD: Okay! I'll make sure it's safe.
ZACHARY: *(One beat.)*
DAD: Are you gonna show us the way?
ZACHARY: *(One beat.)*
DAD: You want me to show you the way.
ZACHARY: *(One beat.)*
DAD: …And you'll follow.
ZACHARY: *(One beat.)*
DAD: Nobody really knows what's out there.
MOM: We'll give it a try.
DAD: To tell you the truth, I kinda like both feet on the ground.
ZACHARY: Dad!
DAD: Okay, okay. Gimme your hand.
> *(Zachary holds drumsticks tight. Turns away. Considers. Looks at Dad. Reluctantly hands him the drumsticks. Considers. Then reaches out his hand to Dad. Smiles. Turns to Mom. Reaches out the other hand.)*
ZACHARY: Mom?
MOM: *(Takes his hand.)* And here's mine.

DAD: *(To Zachary.)* Until you let go.

ZACHARY: Ready for takeoff?

DAD: Fasten your seatbelts.

    (Mom/Dad/Zachary hold hands and lift off. Drumbeat flurries. Music in.)

DAD: Whooooo!

MOM: Ohhhh!

DAD: My heart! My knees! My stomach!

MOM: How far can we go?

DAD: We'll find out...

MOM: Where will we land?

DAD: We'll see...

    (Music in.)

SCENE TWELVE
Zachary's Flight #3

    (Mom/Dad/Zachary glide. All go into flight. Arms uplifted.)

MOM: Beautiful.

DAD: Yeah...

MOM: Quiet...

DAD: Yeah...

MOM: Calm...

DAD: Yeah...

MOM: How long is the flight?

ZACHARY: Who knows...

DAD: Who knows...

    (Mom/Dad and Zachary fly as music soars. Lights indicate they are in space. Music continues to soar as lights fade.)

END OF PLAY

A Dead Man's Apartment
by Edward Allan Baker

This work is dedicated to Jim Wargowsky,
in memory of a gentle man.

BIOGRAPHY

Mr. Baker's plays have been produced all over the United States and Canada and include *Dolores, Rosemary with Ginger, North of Providence, Lady of Fadima, Prairie Avenue, Face Divided, The Buffer, The Bride of Olneyville Square, A Public Street Marriage, 27 Benedict Street,* and *In the Spirit* (co-authored with Native American Ensemble Chuka Lokoli). *Dolores* is published in *Best Short Plays 1988–1989,* and was made into a short film that starred Judith Ivey. He is published by Smith and Kraus, Inc., Dramatists Play Service and Applause Theatre Books.

He has authored over a half a dozen screenplays and is currently working on an adaptation for the screen of his play *Rosemary with Ginger* for Showtime, Inc. He's a member of The Ensemble Studio Theatre, The Dramatists Guild, and Writers Guild, East. He resides in northwest Connecticut with his wife Caroline and three children.

AUTHOR'S NOTE

Writing *A Dead Man's Apartment* was great fun for me. I just got out of its way. The writing Master Ray Bradbury said: "Self-conciousness is the enemy of all art, be it acting, writing, painting, or living itself, which is the greatest art of all."

ORIGINAL PRODUCTION

A Dead Man's Apartment was first produced at The Ensemble Studio Theatre Marathon 1995 One-Act Play Festival. It was directed by Ron Stetson (stage manager, Kelly Corona) with the following cast:

Lonnie	David McConeghey
Valerie	Alexondra Lee
Nickie	Ilene Kristen
Al	Bill Cwikowski

CHARACTERS

LONNIE: 38.

NICKIE: 38.

VALERIE MARIE: 17.

AL: mid-40s.

TIME

Noon-ish, Summer, 1994

PLACE

A 2nd floor apartment in Providence

SETTING

A spacious and sparsely-furnished flat with two windows upstage, shades pulled most of the way down. The door is stage-left. A well-worn couch is center. Mismatched kitchen chairs are here and there. A couple of lamps. A table in a corner with soda bottles, pizza boxes, cereal boxes, and doughnut boxes atop it. A phone and phone answering machine are on the floor close to the couch. A suggestion for preshow music—early Joan Armatrading "To the Limit".

A DEAD MAN'S
APARTMENT

Preshow music and lights fade to black. Pause. Lights up on Lonnie (38), a balding overweight man clad in workman's overalls. He dashes to the phone machine on the floor. He hits the play-button and hears:

MAN'S VOICE: "You're a dead man."
(Lonnie shakes his head.)
LONNIE: Shit… *(He plays it again.)*
MAN'S VOICE: "You're a dead man."
(Lonnie stands up. Paces, nervously.)
LONNIE: Shit, she's gonna know it's me, Goddamn it! Uh… *(He practices Italianstyle)* You're a dead-a man-ah. *(Doesn't like it. Again, louder.)* You…are…a…dead-a man-a! *(Doesn't like it. Runs and grabs a dish towel from the table. Covers his mouth then does it.)* You're a dead man…
(He likes it. Reaches in his pocket for some change while rehearsing the phrase a few more times. He turns to go for the door when it suddenly opens revealing Nickie (38) in sunglasses, baseball cap, and a hardware-store smock. She looks at him. He looks at her.)
NICKIE: Today's the day, Lonnie. I can't do this anymore. I can't pretend that I believe somethin that I don't cause a the kids yunno, they been in the way an I I don't want to be with you anymore, next to you, callin you or or ironin your shirts or cookin your meals. *(She has backed Lonnie to the couch. She rips off her hat, glasses, and*

smock. Drops her pocketbook.) I'm at a place that is kinda hard to explain but I know it's the end of something and I want to get out before I reach forty, okay? I feel sick inside cause of it every day an an at night I sit on the edge of the bed an I see your shape an I hear you snorin and I grab my Saint Jude Medal and I pray for strength, for help, and I say *"Get me the fuck out of this mess!"* I I say it with tears in my eyes and I say it really pissed off an I say it every night. I I have to say it'd be easier in a way if you hit me an the kids but you never did an you always get your ass outta bed in the mornin to go to work to pay the bills...it's just that um...that I don't feel anything deep for you *and I'm so fuckin' bored I could die, do you understand?!*

(Lonnie stirs to get up. She waves him off.)

NICKIE: Wait wait... *(Beat.)* Where are we goin? I'm afraid and I just want to snap my fingers an go forward five years or back twenty. I for a long time have felt my weddin ring is around my neck an gettin tighter an tighter an...

LONNIE: *(Rises.)* Okay Nickie, I...

NICKIE: *Let me go! Just let me go!* Please say "It's all right, I understand, have a good life, good luck, and good-bye." An then just go. Walk away. No no tears. No anger. No hurt feelings. Just...walk... away...from me...

(He waits. She nods. He rises to where she was standing. She sits on the couch. He begins to get out of his overalls and struggles in doing so.)

LONNIE: *(After a nervous moment.)* I'm...goin to leave you...

NICKIE: *(Waits a beat.)* Uh-huh...and...why are...

LONNIE: Cause I've thought it out an I'm...

NICKIE: You're...

LONNIE: Leavin. I thought it out...

NICKIE: What? That's it?

LONNIE: *(Holds his hand up.)* This isn't as easy for me as as it was for you...

NICKIE: You're right, you're right...

LONNIE: *(Continues.)* Uh...I I want to get out of this before I'm forty an I I'm so sick of your shape...in the in our bed, and it makes me sick inside an you're good with the kids an an cookin an you do get up, you know, in the mornin an uh I uh you you do get up, you know in the mornin... *(Lonnie finally steps out of his overalls in the stage left area revealing him in Bermuda shorts, flowery shirt, black socks and sandals.)* An uh you you never hit me an I'd say that's a good thing an…

NICKIE: *(Suspicious.)* Lonnie…

LONNIE: *(Continuing.)* And if I had a Saint medal, I would scream to its face *"Get me the fuck…"*

NICKIE: *(Stands.)* Lonnie!

(He looks at her.)

NICKIE: Are you havin doubts?

LONNIE: *(Lightens up.)* Oh, oh, you're havin doubts?

NICKIE: *No!* I love you Lonnie!

LONNIE: And I love you Nickie!

(They run into each other's arms and kiss passionately.)

NICKIE: Oh God please don't have doubts…

LONNIE: The way you ended tellin your husband uh, "Say it's all right, I understand, have a good life…"

NICKIE: "…good luck an good-bye and then just go, just leave me, no tears, no…"

LONNIE: It won't happen that way.

NICKIE: It might.

LONNIE: If that happened…

NICKIE: I know it won't be easy but…

LONNIE: If that happened…

NICKIE: But it might if…

LONNIE: If that happened…

NICKIE: If he believes I'm…oh I'm sorry. Finish. Finish. "If that happened…"

LONNIE: If that happened, maybe what we have wouldn't be as deep.

NICKIE: "If that happened, maybe what we have wouldn't be as deep."

LONNIE: You know what I'm sayin?

NICKIE: "If that happened, maybe what we…"

LONNIE: Nickie, there's somethin else…

NICKIE: *(Pulls away from him.)* You're not goin to leave her, are you?

LONNIE: Listen to me. I know that leavin my wife an kids is the right thing to do, shit, I felt that the first time I saw you behind the counter of the hardware store but… *(He takes a breath, holds her steady.)* Somebody wants to take me out.

NICKIE: On a date?

LONNIE: No! Take me out like…kill!

NICKIE: Who would want to kill you?

LONNIE: When I got here today I I saw the light on the machine flashing an…well just listen… *(He gets on his knees. He plays it for her.)*

MAN'S VOICE: "You're a dead man."

(Nickie screams out loud. He plays it again.)

MAN'S VOICE: "You're a dead man."

(Nickie gets on her knees next to Lonnie.)

NICKIE: *(Whispers.)* Who the hell could that be?

LONNIE: *(Whispers.)* Is it your husband?

NICKIE: *(Whispers.)* I…do you think it's your wife?

LONNIE: *(Harsh whisper back.)* How the hell could it be my wife?

NICKIE: Maybe she had someone do it.

LONNIE: Could be the same for you.

NICKIE: "Could be the same for you."

LONNIE: Your husband had someone do it.

NICKIE: "Your husband had…"

LONNIE: *(Stands, upset.)* For Chrissakes Nickie, is it or isn't it?!

NICKIE: *(Hurt.)* Lonnie…that's the first time you ever yelled at me.

LONNIE: I'm sorry. Just a little nervous… Uh, death bothers me.

(She stands and hugs him.)

NICKIE: I don't want nothin to happen to you, oh my God…

LONNIE: I know you don't.

NICKIE: If you die…

LONNIE: You'd die.

NICKIE: *(Beat.)* I don't know, I got kids, hon.

LONNIE: *(Turns away.)* Right-right.

NICKIE: Part a me would die, though.

LONNIE: Yup-yup.

NICKIE: *(Goes to him.)* Would you die if I died?

LONNIE: I got kids too.

NICKIE: That's what I'm sayin.

LONNIE: Same thing, uh part a me would die.

NICKIE: That's what I'm sayin so don't be hurt, okay?

(They embrace warmly.)

LONNIE: Do you think it's your husband?

NICKIE: God, no, it couldn't be because how would he know? *(She moves from Lonnie, thinking.)* Unless…

LONNIE: Unless what?

NICKIE: *(Talking to herself.)* Unless she was so mad at me an decided to tell…

LONNIE: *(Cuts her off.)* Who are you talkin about?!

NICKIE: Valerie!

LONNIE: You told your daughter about us?!

(Nickie goes to the door and swings it open, yells out.)

NICKIE: *Valerie Marie!*

(Lonnie runs to Nickie.)

LONNIE: Wait a minute, wait a minute! *(He closes door.)*

NICKIE: Lonnie, it's all right. Me an her, we're like girlfriends… *(She reopens the door, yells out.)* Get up here!

VALERIE: *(From offstage.)* All right!

LONNIE: *(Closes door.)* This is the same girl who tried to kill herself three times?!

NICKIE: Four if you count the toilet bowl incident but…

LONNIE: *(Blocks door.)* I'm very nervous about this…

NICKIE: *(Gets close to him.)* You love me, don't you?

(He nods.)

NICKIE: Then move from the door, c'mon, we're on a lunch break.

(Sudden knocking at the door. Lonnie tenses up.)

LONNIE: Maybe I'll just leave an you play the message for her without me bein here an that way if…

(Nickie grabs Lonnie's face and kisses him, madly, then yanks him from the door. She throws it open and is face-to-face with Valerie Marie .)

NICKIE: Did you tell your father about me an Lonnie?!

VALERIE: *(Dryly.)* Jesus Christ, Ma, is this him?

LONNIE: *(From across the room.)* Hi.

NICKIE: *(Closes door.)* Lonnie, Valerie. Valerie, Lonnie.

(Valerie is clad in baggy jeans, a flannel shirt over a T-shirt, and a baseball cap worn backwards. She stares at Lonnie.)

VALERIE: You a chef or somethin?

NICKIE: I told you he's a mechanic.

VALERIE: He looks like a chef.

NICKIE: He works on fire trucks.

VALERIE: He looks like a chef.

LONNIE: I work on fire trucks.

NICKIE: *(By the phone machine.)* Get over here, Valerie.

VALERIE: *(Eyes on Lonnie.)* So you're the guy with the "big heart."

NICKIE: Listen to this an tell me who it is.

(Nickie plays message.)

MAN'S VOICE: "You're a dead man."

NICKIE: Is that your father?

VALERIE: I can't tell.

NICKIE: Get on the floor an listen again.

(Valerie does. Message replayed.)

MAN'S VOICE: "You're a dead man."

VALERIE: Ma, I can't tell...

NICKIE: Listen again, closer this time...

. *(Nickie holds Valerie's head down to the machine.)*

MAN'S VOICE: "You're a dead man."

VALERIE: No idea.

(Nickie releases Valerie.)

LONNIE: Uh, forget the message for a sec an let me ask you a question if I can. Did you speak to your father about your mother and I?

VALERIE: Whadda you, retarded?

NICKIE: *(Hits Valerie.)* Watch your mouth!

VALERIE: He asked me a retarded question!

NICKIE: It's not a...

LONNIE: *(Interrupts.)* Okay, okay, so you didn't?

NICKIE: You didn't, right?

VALERIE: *(Stands.)* Me an him don't talk. Don't know how to.

NICKIE: *(To Lonnie.)* It's true. They don't.

VALERIE: Once a year on my birthday he gives me a real weak hug.

NICKIE: Well next year on your birthday you're gonna get a hug from the king-of-hugs, right Lonnie? *(Gestures to Lonnie.)* C'mon, give her a hug, c'mon...

VALERIE: *(Backs away.)* Ma, I don't think so...

(Nickie brings Valerie to Lonnie.)

NICKIE: Hug, hug, feel what a real hug is like.

LONNIE: *(To Valerie.)* It's okay, you don't have to...

NICKIE: C'mon.

VALERIE: Some other time.

LONNIE: Sure.

NICKIE: No, now!

LONNIE: Nickie...

NICKIE: Hug...hug, huh, *hug!*

LONNIE: Okay, all right...

(They hug. Nickie stands back to admire.)

NICKIE: This is soooo nice.

LONNIE: We done?

NICKIE: Huh, Val? Somethin, isn't it?

LONNIE: *(Uncomfortable.)* Okay Val…you can…uh Val?

(Valerie has tightened her grip on Lonnie.)

NICKIE: You gotta let go Honey, it's not your birthday, c'mon…

LONNIE: C'mon Val, we got other things to uh do so…

NICKIE: *(Pulling at Valerie.)* You gotta let him go… *(More pulling.)* Valerie…let…the…man…go!

LONNIE: *(Struggles.)* C'mon Valerie…

NICKIE: *(Steps back.)* Oh Christ! Bang her up against the wall!

LONNIE: I'm not gonna bang her up against the…

NICKIE: God I love you! You're so sensitive…

(She kisses Lonnie passionately then tries again to pry Valerie loose from Lonnie.)

NICKIE: Valerie Marie, stop actin like a pit bull an let the man go!

(Valerie hangs tighter.)

LONNIE: Val? Can you hear us? Can she hear us?

NICKIE: *(Again, backs off.)* Oh I can't believe this. I am so embarrassed. Uh I'll be right back.

(She dashes to the door. Lonnie follows her with Valerie attached to him.)

LONNIE: Where the hell you goin?!

NICKIE: *(At the door, opens it.)* I gotta get my brother… *(She is gone.)*

LONNIE: No! *(He yells out the door.)* I'll bang her up against the wall! Nickie! *(Silence. He closes the door.)* Great. *(He moves deeper into the flat with Valerie attached to him.)* You want somethin? Doughnut? Soda?

VALERIE: *(Muffled.)* Diet?

LONNIE: Yeah.

VALERIE: I hate diet soda.

(He paces some.)

LONNIE: You really should let go now.

VALERIE: I don't want to.

LONNIE: Why?

VALERIE: I don't know why.

LONNIE: You don't know why?

VALERIE: I don't know why.

(Lonnie paces around the room with Valerie attached to him.)

LONNIE: Uh okay but just a little thing that kinda bothers me… *(He ambles over to the window and peers out.)* I'm a little nervous today about a lot of things an added to that as of right now is your uncle comin in here an seein you attached to me. I don't think it's how we should first meet, you know what I'm sayin?

VALERIE: *(Suddenly lets him go.)* I'm not stupid!

LONNIE: *(Relieved.)* And I'm not saying you are. You look very stable to me.

(She takes a step closer to him and screams at him, insanely.)

VALERIE: You're just like everybody else! Just like those assholes in school sayin shit like, "Don't fuck, don't smoke, don't wear hats, don't drink and drive!" Don't-don't don't! Meanwhile... *(She pauses, looks at him.)* You listening to me?

(He nods.)

VALERIE: Meanwhile, the TV and magazines are sayin, "Drink! Smoke! Fuck! Drive this car! Image is everything!"

(Valerie is pacing like a maddened animal, fists clenched. Lonnie eyes her.)

VALERIE: I am so sick of it, so so so sick of being pulled an pulled pulled! I am so so sick...of...it!

(She scoops up a bag of Oreo cookies from the table then plops down on the couch. Lonnie inches toward her. She opens a cookie and begins eating the icing, slowly.)

VALERIE: After I quit school I was watchin talk shows like oh probly uh maybe I don't know...ten, twelve a day cause I had the house to myself... *(Eats the cookie.)* Then...I got so fuckin bored at these these assholes on TV that I...*Miss Stupid*...decided I would look an look for stuff my parents had hidden away from me an me *Miss Stupid* found these notebooks a my mother's an I, man, I hit the jackpot, lemme tell ya...*(Leans forward.)* I know all about you.

LONNIE: What do you know a...?

VALERIE: I know about the cyst you had on your...

LONNIE: *(Quickly.)* It was a birthmark.

VALERIE: I know you hate mushrooms. Shellfish. Ham. Chi-chi beans. I know you think your death will come by drowning.

LONNIE: That's changin but um...

VALERIE: I know you cried the time my mother gave you the first back rub you ever had.

LONNIE: *(Worriedly.)* You didn't show your father those notebooks, did you? I mean I don't know you so I have to...

VALERIE: *(Snaps.)* Fuck him! As soon as I got tits we stopped talkin. He's nothin but a shadow who can piss an I don't give him the time of day. *(She gets on the floor next to the machine. She plays the message.)*

MAN'S VOICE: "You're a dead man."

VALERIE: Could be him.

LONNIE: Uh yeah could be him, but listen…

VALERIE: Has reason.

LONNIE: Uh-huh yeah, um…

VALERIE: But I don't know.

LONNIE: But you said he "has reason."

VALERIE: *(Looks up at him.)* Could be him.

LONNIE: Okay okay, lemme ask you this, uh, has he ever…has he ever hurt anyone before?

VALERIE: "Has he ever…has he ever hurt anyone before?"

LONNIE: You know, gettin jealous and hit. Shoot. Beat up.

VALERIE: Have you?

LONNIE: No.

VALERIE: You fuckin whacked your son one time, didn't you?

LONNIE: What? How did you know that?

VALERIE: *(Coyly.)* He told me.

LONNIE: *(Aghast.)* You talked with my son?!

(Door bursts open. Nickie re-enters with Brother Al (45ish) right behind her.)

NICKIE: Oh good, she's off a him!

AL: This him?

NICKIE: Al, Lonnie. Lonnie, Al.

(An exchange of vague nods. Nickie goes to Lonnie.)

NICKIE: No need to be nervous, Lonnie. Al only wants what's good for me.

LONNIE: Good good, that's good.

(Al is a tough-looking man clad in jeans, tight T-shirt that displays his muscles. He wears work boots. He is eating a sandwich and carrying a metal lunch box. He is fixed on Lonnie as Nickie bends to the phone machine.)

NICKIE: Ready Al?

AL: Hit it.

(She does.)

MAN'S VOICE: "You're a dead man."

NICKIE: Did you hear it, Al?

AL: *(Looking at Lonnie.)* I was chewin too loud. Hit it again.

(She does.)

MAN'S VOICE: "You're a dead man."

LONNIE: Boy do I hate hearin that.

AL: Don't blame ya...

NICKIE: What do you think, Al?

AL: I think someone's out to kill him.

NICKIE: No shit, Al, do you know who it is?

AL: I don't give a shit who it is, they're not tryin to kill me... *(Looks at Lonnie.)* But it'd scare me, I know that.

(Lonnie goes to Nickie, pulls her aside to talk.)

LONNIE: Okay okay then let's...Nickie, let's just back off for today or for a coupla days an then we'll...

NICKIE: *No!* You can't do this to me!

LONNIE: Listen, just until...

NICKIE: No!

LONNIE: ...until we let things settle down...

NICKIE: Cause you'll go back to her an probly pick another hardware store to go to an that'll be it!

LONNIE: Calm down, calm down...

(Al snaps his fingers to get Valerie with him and makes to the door.)

AL: Let's go, Nickie...

NICKIE: No! Lonnie, tell Al what you told me that time we was flyin kites...

VALERIE: *(Smugly.)* "I never felt this strong for anybody in my whole life."

NICKIE: *(Stunned.)* How did you know that?

VALERIE: Your notebooks, Ma.

AL: *(Bemusedly.)* You two was flyin kites?

VALERIE: "I want a man to kiss me forever."

NICKIE: *(Goes to Val.)* Two can play this game.

VALERIE: "I want a man to wake me up just to hold me tight."

NICKIE: "I love it when Greg looks at my chest!"

VALERIE: *(Stunned.)* You read my diary?!

NICKIE: "I'd sleep with Larry in two seconds if he asked!"

VALERIE: "I feel so hungry for somethin I can't explain!"

NICKIE: *(Face to face with Val.)* "I wanna scream out *I itch so bad I can't sleep!*"

AL: *Hey! Separate!*

(The girls part quickly. Slight pause.)

LONNIE: *(Finally.)* So look...we're all on a lunch break here an-an...

(He inches his way along the back wall toward the door.) Time's runnin out so why don't we go back to work an...

AL: *(In Lonnie's way.)* You still thinkin a breakin with your wife tonight?

NICKIE: *(Goes to Lonnie.)* Yes he is! Tell him Lonnie! Say yes-you-are!

LONNIE: Well so much has happened and I...

(Nickie pushes Lonnie up against the wall.)

NICKIE: I need you. I need your life in my life, oh please don't back from our promises...

AL: Anythin the two of you had is by the boards cause the man is scared a losin his wife...

LONNIE: Life.

AL: What?

LONNIE: You said "scared a losin his wife" but you meant life.

NICKIE: Oh God Lonnie, are you ascared a losin your wife?

LONNIE: Life!

AL: *(Closes in on Lonnie.)* But if you really loved Nickie, you'd do right by her, right or wrong?

NICKIE: And he's goin to, right Lonnie?

VALERIE: God Ma, stop slobbering.

AL: Let the man speak.

(All look at Lonnie.)

LONNIE: *(After a beat.)* I do...I do love Nickie. We've had some fun.

AL: Right-right, flyin kites.

(Lonnie moves to the back of the couch, looks down at Nickie who is seated.)

LONNIE: Uh, eating out.

VALERIE: Shitload a that I bet.

(Nickie makes a move to go at Valerie but Lonnie holds her shoulders.)

AL: *(Moves in on Lonnie.)* So basic sneaking around, cheatin, screwin around with another man's wife, tellin her things you can't tell your wife an doin things you don't do with your wife an an...

(Lonnie is backing from Al, Al stalks him while speaking.)

AL: You take your wife to the show? Out to eat?

LONNIE: No. I used to.

AL: An your wife's a housewife, right Val?

VALERIE: Yup.

AL: An Nickie she's givin you a a what? A glow kinda in your gut? A feelin that gets you through a day? It makes bein next to your wife uh harder or easier?

LONNIE: Little a both but listen…

AL: No you listen! There are families involved! Kids. Picture albums. Ma-mentoes. In-laws. Bank accounts. Kids. You take your boys fishin?

LONNIE: *(Still backing up.)* What?

AL: Bowlin?

LONNIE: No, I…

AL: Ball games?

LONNIE: Uh no…

AL: Two boys, right? Right, Val?

VALERIE: *(Enjoying this.)* Ten and sixteen.

AL: You go to church?

NICKIE: I love you Lonnie…

LONNIE: *(To Al.)* No I…

VALERIE: *(Right behind Al.)* His son says he listens to tapes um somethin like "unlocking your inner doorknob."

LONNIE: When did you talk to my son?

VALERIE: Last week.

LONNIE: Did you know this Nickie?

NICKIE: *(From the couch.)* I didn't think it would hurt.

LONNIE: We had an agreement not to tell anybody about us!

NICKIE: Lonnie Hon, it's been so nice I couldn't keep it in.

AL: So okay you're listening to tapes. Uh, Val tells me your son says you're moody, sorta lazy, like to smoke grass in the basement.

VALERIE: Can't fix anythin but cars an wanders winda to winda.

AL: No shit?

VALERIE: Plays gospel music real loud and cries.

AL: *(To Lonnie.)* That true?

(Al and Valerie have Lonnie cornered in upstage right corner.)

LONNIE: I don't believe this…

AL: Hey pal, you started this! An I gotta know if you got the insides to go through life with my sista. That fair soundin to you or do you got a problem with me?

NICKIE: Be careful, Lonnie…

(Lonnie backs farther into the corner.)

LONNIE: No, I do have a problem with you. I have a problem now that I know my son was talked to an an I got a problem with the surprise of you an an Valerie bein here today an…

VALERIE: Don't forget the death threat.

LONNIE: An that gospel music thing happened one time!

AL: Can't forget someone's on to you.

(Valerie pulls Al to the side to talk with him.)

VALERIE: His son says that he disappears to the fuckin basement when somethin goes wrong or something like "when he feels cornered."

(Again Lonnie is trying to inch his way to the door. Nickie notices and runs to block the doorway.)

NICKIE: Tell 'em Lonnie that we're goin to a place that'll have no basement an tell 'em you're gonna change with me an you'll be different, c'mon, tell 'em...

(Pause. Lonnie is motionless.)

NICKIE: C'mon...tell 'em...

(Lonnie remains unblinkingly still. Nickie rubs his face in a loving manner.)

NICKIE: Okay then, let's tell 'em together, okay? You wanna do that? Tell 'em together?

(Lonnie nods, barely. Al and Valerie laugh and move to sit and eat together. Nickie coaxes Lonnie, pulling him toward Al and Valerie.)

NICKIE: Nickie and I we...we...

LONNIE: *(Softly.)* Take walks...

NICKIE: Holdin hands an...

LONNIE: An she loves lookin at horses. So we do that...

NICKIE: An we eat...

LONNIE AND NICKIE: Clamcakes...

LONNIE: *(Gaining energy.)* On the rocks a Narragansett...

NICKIE: Not lettin the spray a the waves bother us...and we talk...

LONNIE: To each other...

NICKIE AND LONNIE: Every day...

LONNIE: An then gettin a place hidden away an an the phone an machine was to have in case one of us couldn't get here...

NICKIE: Cause a some family thing...

LONNIE: We decided to do that...

(Al and Valerie stare at them in quiet disbelief.)

NICKIE: An then we set a date to tell our, which is today an uh...

LONNIE: *(Cuts in.)* An then this message kinda made me look, uh think at what we intend to do uh real hard an...uh...

(Nickie whispers something to him. Moves behind Valerie and Al.)

LONNIE: Uh...I went with Nickie to her father's grave an I stood there in the rain an watched her cry an bend to smooth the stone with her hand...

(*Awkward silence for a beat. Al is waiting.*)

NICKIE: An you said...when I came back to the car, you said...

LONNIE: Oh-oh. I said it looked like she was rubbin his face...

NICKIE: (*Leans to Al and Valerie.*) Isn't that nice?

(*Nothing from Al and Valerie.*)

LONNIE: I felt something for her in a place I never been to before an...

(*Lowers his head. He begins to cry, softly.*)

VALERIE: You never been to a graveyard?

NICKIE: (*Moved.*) Oh Lonnie... (*She is comforting him.*)

AL: Whoa-whoa is he bawlin?

NICKIE: I told you he was sensitive.

AL: (*To Valerie.*) Is he fuckin bawlin?!

VALERIE: (*Goes to look.*) He's fuckin bawlin.

AL: (*Stands up.*) Don't let me see you bawlin, pal, cause I'll whack you!

NICKIE: Cut it out Al!

AL: An worse than that is a woman goin, "Oh he's so sensitive, I think I'll love him!"

NICKIE: He's all upset cause a that...

(*Gestures to phone machine. Lonnie is trying to recover.*)

AL: This is it?!

(*Nickie is wiping Lonnie's face with a Kleenex.*)

NICKIE: Take a breath, Lon-Hon...

AL: (*Pacing.*) This guy is what you want?! So you can go an fly kites an cry together?! This is what blowin my lunch hour is been about?! I thought I was comin to meet a man!

NICKIE: You're not seein the real Lonnie!

(*She sits Lonnie down on the couch.*)

AL: (*Goes at Lonnie.*) Whadda you goin to do when her son gets outta drug rehab an needs you? Whadda you goin to do when Val here comes screamin to you for answers? You goin to start cryin? You goin to say, "the hell with this," an go back to your wife? You goin to give 'em the wrong answers?!

NICKIE: (*Gets between Al and Lonnie.*) Stop it Al! You don't understand, he's more than what you're gettin today on account a that damn message an...

AL: (*Moves by Nickie.*) Do you think leavin your wife for Nickie is goin to make you smart all of a sudden?

NICKIE: He's not lookin to be smart!

VALERIE: "He's not lookin to be smart!"

(Lonnie is feeling the bombardment as he slouches down on the couch.)

LONNIE: Stop…look…just just…please just…

(Al has had enough. He picks up his lunch box and makes for the door. Nickie runs and stops him before he can exit.)

NICKIE: Listen to me, Al, this is the man I I want an I know you're seein just the outside an an…look at me Al!

(Al does.)

NICKIE: I need him…I'm so afraid of…of turnin into a dried up woman, like Ma, yunno?

AL: *(Points a finger at her.)* Hey!

(He attempts to leave but Nickie swipes his lunch box.)

NICKIE: Look at me Al an I'm askin you to go deep down an an understand why I need Lonnie an…an then, let us go. Let me feel a man's hand on my face again. Look at me Al…

(He does.)

NICKIE: I'm so tired a standin still. I I want the warmth…Lonnie's warmth to move me inside to bein happy.

(She hands him back his lunch box then rejoins Lonnie on the couch. They hold hands. Al takes a full moment to eye the both of them on the couch. He looks straight at Lonnie.)

AL: Is this a dick thing?

LONNIE: What?

AL: This has got to be a dick thing, right?

NICKIE: We haven't even had sex!

AL: *(To Lonnie.)* True?

LONNIE: True.

VALERIE: Wonda if the person who wants to kill ya knows that?

LONNIE: *(To Al.)* All we been doin in here is is kissin on the couch an talkin about uh life an dreamin a bein together, of of another life together!

AL: Oh that sounds like alotta fun…

(Al walks away from them. He is thinking. All wait for his next word. Finally—)

AL: Val, do your thing?

LONNIE: What? What thing?

AL: *(To Valerie.)* Kinda like the shit you did to me last week.

NICKIE: *(Rises from the couch.)* Oh shit…

VALERIE: The uh I-don't-wanna-live-no-more or the-bangin-the-head-up-against-the-wall?

AL: Go with the I-don't-wanna-live-no-more.

(Valerie starts to hyperventilate, getting ready.)

NICKIE: Do your best Lonnie.

LONNIE: Best at what?!

AL: *(Instructs Lonnie.)* Okay so now you're in the parlor…An an say you an Nickie are a "thing" now an an Val comes outta somewhere all upset an has no one else to go to but you…

LONNIE: *(To Nickie.)* Why did you bring them here?!

AL: *(Walking away.)* You can't cash in nothin and get somethin!

LONNIE: What the hell does that mean?!

NICKIE: I love you Lonnie…

LONNIE: Then why are you doin this?!

VALERIE: *(Next to Al.)* Can I start now?

NICKIE: *(Rushes to Lonnie on the couch.)* Listen to me, you can do it. Prove to them we can and will be happy before our lunch break is up.

(Al moves Nickie away from Lonnie just as Valerie jumps on the couch then leans into Lonnie's face.)

VALERIE: I want to die! I can't see any reason to get up anymore!

LONNIE: Nickie, I'm hurtin…

VALERIE: My mother just says, "Do what I say!" An my father says, "Get off the couch I gotta lay down." An every day is the same an I…

LONNIE: Nickie…

VALERIE: Maybe people will feel for me when I'm dead—*The pain of livin will be over*—

LONNIE: Nickie, why can't we just go on the way we been goin?!

NICKIE: *(Goes to Lonnie.)* Lonnie, your face is flushed… *(To Al.)* I never seen that before.

AL: *(Bends to Lonnie.)* Never mind her, what are you goin to say to Val?!

VALERIE: *(Still atop Lonnie.)* A knife in my heart, a rope around my neck…

LONNIE: I have no idea what you're doin!

VALERIE: *(Looks at Al.)* Should I stop?

AL: No, keep goin Val!

NICKIE: Start fightin Lonnie Honey!

VALERIE: I don't wanna live oh stepfather an I need to hear from somebody on why I should, okay?!

LONNIE: *(In her face.)* Well, *fuck you,* okay?!

VALERIE: Gimme a reason oh stepfather for seein the sun come up tammara!

(Lonnie struggles to get off the couch.)

LONNIE: Oh for Chrissakes…

(He turns around to face Valerie who is standing on the couch.)

VALERIE: I-I…look I bit my wrist open an it's bleedin, hurry I'm bleedin bad…

LONNIE: You're not bleedin!

VALERIE: *(Holds out her wrist.)* My blood…it's drippin on your feet, it's gettin…I'm gettin…I'm feelin so so weak…

(She falls into Lonnie's arms. Lonnie lays her down on the couch.)

LONNIE: I don't know what to tell you…I got through it. We all get through it. You do what you have to do and you get through it an yeah yeah most of it sucks but you push on, push on past the beatin's and the bein ignored an push past no one there to hold you an you fuckin push on past when you think you don't matta an nothin matters an there's no peace in anybody's fuckin house! For Chrissakes people dyin for gettin laid an other people dyin cause they can't get laid an you kids…you Goddamn kids nowadays… you want all the answers like right away! "Gimme an answer or I'll kill myself!" *Well fuck you!* You don't think we had…we adults had pain when we was growin up?! For Chrissakes *wake the fuck up* an be thankful you got a roof over ya head an food on the table an a bed to wallow over your bullshit in! Be thankful for the malls you hang out in an for the stupid clothes ya wear an the teachers you insult and hate!

(Valerie gets up from the couch to cross the room and is stopped by Lonnie who spins her around to face him. He shakes her.)

LONNIE: Just know that all this will pass, Goddamn it, all…of… this…will…pass!

(Silence. Valerie walks to Nickie.)

VALERIE: *(Looks at Lonnie.)* Oh yeah, I really wanna live now.

LONNIE: *(Turns around to Al.)* Don't you agree? I mean these kids, they gotta be told an I'm sick a them thinkin they can say whatever they want an…

(Al presses down on the machine with his foot.)

MAN'S VOICE: "You're a dead man."

(A slight pause. Lonnie turns to Nickie.)

LONNIE: Nickie, say somethin, tell 'em our love is in this apartment an how much we shared...

VALERIE: Ma, he's the worst one of the whole bunch.

(Lonnie's face drops.)

LONNIE: What? What did you say?

AL: Lon-man, it's all over.

LONNIE: *(Angrily.)* Hey, technically speaking, this is our apartment an I could kick your ass outta here or call the cops!

AL: *(Gets closer to Lonnie.)* I own this building, pal! So technically speaking I'm your landlord an I let Nickie use it when she thinks someone like you is the *one* to save her. Shit, I could name five, six guys in the past...

NICKIE: Don't...

AL: I won't honey...

(Nickie crosses to the upstage table to get the picture of Lonnie and her.)

NICKIE: Poor Lonnie... *(She removes the photo.)*

AL: It's all over between you an my sista.

LONNIE: I'm not gonna let this happen.

AL: What are you gonna do?

(Lonnie runs to Nickie and picks her up, holds her in a bear hug.)

LONNIE: Oh God Nickie it's been so nice that no matta what was goin on in my home life, I always knew I had this an an you...

AL: Let her go...

NICKIE: *(Struggling.)* Lonnie, let me go...

LONNIE: What we had was fine til...

AL: *(Pulling at Lonnie.)* It's over, let her go!

NICKIE: I I can't breathe...

(Valerie is helping Al to get Lonnie to release Nickie.)

LONNIE: I need you to hold me on Tuesdays an Thursdays an an lets add on Sundays, okay?

AL: *(Pulls harder at Lonnie.)* C'mon, that's enough...let go...

NICKIE: *(Barely audible.)* I...please...Lon...

(Al gets close to Lonnie's ear.)

AL: I killed a man in this apartment!

(Lonnie looks at Nickie. She nods. Lonnie puts Nickie down, releases her.)

AL: A man who was screwin my wife. Name unimportant. I stabbed him beyond repair.

(Nickie is at the table with Valerie touching up her makeup.)

AL: I watched them from the building across the street. I saw him massaging her breasts, the same breasts I kissed when she was seventeen...those were my breasts! His tongue in her ear, that was *my* ear! She was doin it with this bum afta she found out I screwed a friend a hers which I could not help by the way, I mean I spent so much time fanta-sizin about her that the first time alone with her I...well it was easy to get started cause I had done her so many times in my head but...uh shit, where was I goin with this?

VALERIE: Killin the bum.

NICKIE: "...his tongue in her ear that was my ear..."

AL: Right. So I went nuts. I I came runnin over here and kicked in the door an so he turned, saw me, pulled up his fly an ran over to the winda an I...I...

NICKIE: Hurry, Al, hurry...

AL: It happened fast an uh funny the things ya rememba but I rememba he he smelled like her...her smell was all over him...Shall-la-mar... *(Lost for a beat.)* Uh I did my time, my crime-of-passion time, an I a course lost her, a course. She's married now to Paul Morretti...

NICKIE: Morretti of Morretti's pizza...

VALERIE: The one on Pontiac Avenue, that one...

NICKIE: *(Caringly.)* Al, don't drive down there no more, you hear me?

AL: Yeah...I uh...my two kids I don't see no more yunno cut off from that an now I protect Nickie from guys like you Lon-man. All you guys, right? All you guys who wanna be safe with somebody but got nothin but what? Dirty laundry? You can't help her but yunno, I don't blame ya, lookit Nickie, she's beautiful, right? She looks like she's twenty years old for Chrissakes, an an her heart up in her eyes an those teeth, the smile of of niceness...

(Nickie beams. Valerie is bored. Lonnie drained.)

NICKIE: Al Hon, c'mon I don't wanna get fired.

AL: *(Goes to Lonnie.)* But hey, I love the thing about the tape you listen to...the...uh...

VALERIE: "Unlocking your inner doorknob" but c'mon Uncle Al, lets...

AL: *(Cuts her off.)* That's a new one, shit, betta than the mailman who said he and Nickie were lovers in a past life in uh...

NICKIE: Mongolia.

AL: *(Laughs.)* Ain't that a winna! Fuckin Mongolia!

(Al, Nickie and Valerie have a good laugh. When it dies down they all look to Lonnie alone on the couch. Al goes and sits next to him.)

AL: Cheer up Lonnie, I maybe saved your life cause hey who knows maybe if you and Nickie say got together an one night you an she have a spat an you get to feelin a little homesick an you circle your old house an there's a car in the driveway you recognize an you start to burn inside real hot in the gut an memories from in that house start to surface yunno, holidays, birthdays, monopoly, an you look in the winda an you see her sittin there lookin the best she's looked in years an there's a guy on the couch next to her, an he's smilin an she's smilin… *(Al takes a moment then—)* Are you ready to see somebody goin afta your wife the way you been goin afta Nickie?

LONNIE: *(Pauses a moment.)* No.

VALERIE: *(At the door.)* Good. Can we get outta here now?

NICKIE: *(Goes to Lonnie.)* So I guess this is… *(Stops looks to Al.)* Hey, what about the "you're a dead man" guy?

AL: Tell her Lonnie.

LONNIE: Uh…it's me. I'm the "you're a dead man" guy.

NICKIE: You threatened your own life?!

LONNIE: I did it to stall the breakin up with my wife cause I wanted to keep things the way they were with me an you…

VALERIE: *(Steps up to Lonnie.)* Well this was fun. Nice to meet ya.

LONNIE: *(Shakes her hand.)* Yeah.

VALERIE: *(Leans into him.)* Don't hit your son no more.

(Lonnie nods understandingly. Nickie steps up to Lonnie.)

NICKIE: Well Lonnie…no tears…

LONNIE: No uh…anger.

NICKIE: No hurt feelings.

LONNIE: Just good-bye.

NICKIE: Good luck.

(They shake hands. Nickie turns to leave with Valerie.)

NICKIE: Oh Jesus Val, did you rememba to turn the sauce down to low before you…

VALERIE: *(Out the door.)* Yeah yeah afta I heard it bubblin.

NICKIE: *(Exits behind Val.)* Your father will have a ca-nip-tion if it's ruined…

AL: It's past lunch, Lon-Man, I don't wanna lose my job. Go home. Tell your wife you lo…

LONNIE: *(Cuts him off.)* Al, don't tell me what I should tell my wife. I know what I should tell my wife.

AL: *(Smiles.)* Now you know. That's somethin, right? *(Gets closer to Lonnie.)* Am I right? Huh? C'mon, am I right? Look at me...

LONNIE: *(Looks at Al, smiles.)* Yeah yeah ya sonofabitch, you're right.

AL: Good. Good.

(Al quickly hugs Lonnie, and cries in his arms. Lonnie comforts him—Al pulls away, he got it out. He proceeds to the door then proclaims—)

AL: I feel good.

(Al exits. Lonnie closes the door then turns back into the room very much a man alive.)

LONNIE: "Now you know. That's something, right?"

(Lights fade as Gospel music is heard coming up and blackout on A Deadman's Apartment.*)*

END OF PLAY

Sonny DeRee's Life Flashes Before His Eyes
by Bill Bozzone

Bill Bozzone dedicates Sonny DeRee's Life *to his parents who, if they were alive, probably wouldn't care for it.*

BIOGRAPHY

Bill Bozzone has been a member of The Ensemble Studio Theatre for the past 16 years. During that time, his plays have included *Rose Cottages, Korea, House Arrest, Saxophone Music, The Second Coming, Fasting, Cosmo's In Love, Good Honest Food, Buck Fever,* and others. Original work has also been produced by Showtime's Act One, Philadelphia Festival Theatre, Manhattan Punch Line, City Theatre of Pittsburgh, and at the Eugene O'Neill National Playwrights Conference. As a screenwriter, Bill Bozzone wrote the feature film, *Full Moon In Blue Water,* and co-wrote the *Ace* nominated teleplay *The Last Elephant.* He lives in Connecticut with his wife, fiction writer Tricia Bauer.

AUTHOR'S NOTE

My own mother was a lot like Emma. A real manipulator. It was pretty much just the two of us after my father died (I was eighteen), and I had no reason to believe she'd ever release her choke hold on me and let me have a separate life. She died of lung cancer three years later, and I still remember the feeling of relief, the sense of absolute freedom, the realization that my life was mine to do with whatever I wished.

I wanted Sonny to reach that same awareness by the end of this play, even though *his* mother—as healthy as a goat—will probably outlive us all.

ORIGINAL PRODUCTION

Sonny DeRee's Life Flashes Before His Eyes was first produced at the Ensemble Studio Theatre Marathon 1995, 18th Annual Festival of One-Act Plays. It was directed by Keith Reddin (stage manager Tamlyn Freund) with the following cast:

Sonny DeRee	Joseph Siravo
Mick Reilly	Holter Graham
Emma DeRee	Suzanne Shepherd

CHARACTERS

SONNY DEREE: 45, a bookmaker. Unsuccessful at just about everything he's ever tried. Not an evil man, just a nonentity.

MICK: 24, a hired killer who, a year ago, was unhappily employed at a Blimpies Sandwich Shop in midtown Manhattan.

EMMA DEREE: 65, Sonny's mom. A widow of one year, she runs a "bait and tackle" shop in Wildwood, New Jersey.

SETTING

A motel room somewhere off the Jersey Turnpike.

SONNY DeRee's LIFE FLASHES BEFORE HIS EYES

Fall. Late afternoon. Sonny DeRee's residence—a cheap motel room somewhere off the New Jersey Turnpike. There are ledger books everywhere—on the desk, on homemade shelves over the desk, stacked in corners. There's a half-full bottle of scotch and two upturned glasses on the dresser. Sonny, 45, paces by the bed while he talks on the phone. He's balding. He·wears slacks and a sweat-stained white shirt. There's a phone book on the bottom shelf of the phone stand. Mick, 24, sits on the straight-backed desk chair and watches. Mick has a buzz cut, a goatee, a number of earrings, tattoos. He wears chinos and a vest over a T-shirt. He holds a chain saw on his lap which he carefully oils and cleans with a handkerchief.

SONNY: *(Into the phone.)*…yeah! Right! Sonny DeRee! From P.S. 181! We sat next to one another in Earth Science! *(He listens.)* Right! Cangelosi's class! *(beat)* Good, and you?! *(Short pause.)* Andrew, listen, I don't have a lot of time to reminisce, so let me get right to the point. I need nine-thousand dollars and I need it like immediately…*(Pause.)* Andrew? *(Sonny sighs, hangs up, puts the phone down.)* This is ridiculous. You might as well kill me right now.

MICK: Okay. *(Mick stands, grabs the pull-cord on the chain saw.)*

SONNY: No! Wait! I didn't mean that! What I mean is, give me a little more time! Another couple of hours! Something could still come through!

MICK: Like what?

SONNY: I don't know! Something!

MICK: Time is a problem for me, Sonny. It really is. Metallica is playing the Forum tonight and I haven't even picked up my ticket.

SONNY: What has that got to do with anything?!

MICK: I kill you right now, I'm out of here in five minutes, I avoid the headaches of rush hour.

(Sonny indicates the chain saw.)

SONNY: Why do you have to use that thing? Why can't you conduct business with a gun like everybody else?!

MICK: The chain saw is my trademark, Sonny. It's something I'm associated with. People see the hit, they see the condition of the deceased, they say, "This looks like Mick Reilly was here."

SONNY: *(approaches)* Mick. Listen. You and I have been pretty close friends over the years.

MICK: We have?

SONNY: Come on, man. We've broken bread together. We've confided. We been like brothers. *(Mick shrugs.)* Donnie-Boy's wedding reception. Did we or did we not hang out together the entire time?

MICK: I didn't even know you were there.

SONNY: Of course I was there! You remember! I kept trying to bum a cigarette off you! Except that you knew I was trying to quit and you wouldn't give me one!

MICK: I was looking out for your health.

SONNY: Yes!

MICK: Ironic, huh?

SONNY: Please, Mick. Lend me the nine grand.

MICK: I can't do that, Sonny. What kind of hitman would I be if I did that? It would set a negative example. It would encourage other people in the future. I would be less like a hired killer and more like Phil Rizzuto of the Money Store.

SONNY: Okay, forget the money! How about this! You could *say* you killed me and who would know? I'd leave the state! I swear to God! Nobody would ever hear a peep from me again!

MICK: I can't do that.

SONNY: Why not?!

MICK: Because this is my job, Sonny. I do it to the best of my ability. *(Pause.)* You know where I was 13 months ago? Blimpies. And friends would come in—my own sister would come in—and expect something for nothing. But I never played that, Sonny. People with me always get what they pay for. No more, no less.

SONNY: *(Nervous laugh.)* I'd like to think I'm a little more important than extra dressing on a wedge.

MICK: You'd like to, but in this case, you're not. *(Pause.)* So. Anything you want before I start? Glass of water, couple of Tylenol?

SONNY: One more phone call. *(Sonny quickly moves to the phone book.)*

MICK: Come on, Sonny. You've already called everybody.

SONNY: Not everybody. *(Sonny pages frantically through the book.)* I saw a name in here last night. "DeRay." Could be a slight variation of my own. Some distant relative.

MICK: *(Approaches.)* Sonny, have a heart. Fifteen more minutes and I hit the Newark Airport crowd.

SONNY: Just take a minute.

MICK: I don't mean to harp on this, but I have a certain phobia when it comes to traffic. Relates to my father who was himself killed on the Long Island Expressway. *(Sonny finds the name in the book.)* Ironically, he was on foot at the time. *(Sonny starts to dial.)* His car had broken down and he was looking for help, and I guess he wasn't paying attention to where he was walking. Wandered right out in front of a bus and was squashed like a tomato. *(Sonny waits.)* Teaches you a valuable lesson, though. *(Pause.)* If you ever break down on the Long Island Expressway? Stay with your vehicle.

SONNY: *(Into phone.)* Hello?! Who is this?! *(Listens.)* "Janine." *(Beat.)* Is your mommy or daddy home, Janine? *(Beat.)* He is. *(Beat.)* He's sleeping. *(Beat.)* Could you wake him up for me, please? *(Beat.)* Why not? *(Beat.)* Janine, honey, this is very important. I promise he won't get mad. *(Beat.)* Because I just know. *(Beat.)* Because he would want you to wake him up. *(Beat.) Because I'm Dying, Janine! (Mick goes to Sonny, takes the phone receiver from him.)*

MICK: That's it.

SONNY: *(Into phone as Mick takes it away.)* You hear that man, Janine?! He has a chain saw! *Don't make me send him over to your house tonight while you're sleeping, Janine…! (Mick hangs up the phone.)*

MICK: Let's just do it. *(Mick takes the saw, yanks the pull cord. The saw comes to life. Mick takes a step or two toward Sonny who falls on his knees, closes his eyes, brings his hands together.)*

SONNY: *(To himself.)* Hail Mary, full of grace, the Lord is with thee… *(Mick stops, turns off the saw. Sonny stops praying, looks up.)* What?!

MICK: I just had a bizarre thought.

SONNY: Tell me!

MICK: Last night? After I got home? There wasn't much on television so I watched this PBS thing. About Neptune. You know. The planet? *(Beat.)* And on Neptune, times goes much slower. Because it travels a larger orbit around the sun. *(Beat.)* In fact, it takes 165 Earth years to make up one Neptune year. If you lived to be 165 years old on earth, you'd still be waiting for your first birthday on Neptune. *(Pause.)* I mean, it just now hit me that if we were on Neptune, you'd still have at least three days before I'd even come by. *(Pause.)* Just a bizarre thought. *(Mick reaches for the pull cord. He hesitates, stops. He listens. Outside, the sound of a car pulling in.)* Now what? *(Mick with the chain saw, walks to the window. Sonny rises, follows him. They both look through the blinds. Outside, the sound of a car door slamming.)*

SONNY: *(Beat.)* I don't believe this.

(Mick looks over at Sonny.)

MICK: Who is it?

SONNY: It's my mother.

MICK: Your mother?

SONNY: I haven't seen this woman in over ten years!

MICK: I can't kill you with her out there!

(There's a knock on the door.)

EMMA: *(Offstage.)* Sonny?!

MICK: Get rid of her!

EMMA: *(Offstage.)* Sonny!

(Sonny opens the door. Emma DeRee, a woman in her sixties, enters. She wears sun glasses, clam diggers, sandals, a blouse. She carries a zippered canvas beach bag.)

SONNY: Christ, Emma. What the hell are you doing here?

EMMA: Molly Santare phoned me this morning. From the old neighborhood. Said she got a call from you last night asking for nine-thousand dollars. She said, that you said, that if you didn't get it you'd be killed. *(Emma removes the sunglasses.)* So here I am. All the way up from Wildwood.

MICK: How was traffic?

(Emma looks over at Mick.)

EMMA: And you are...?

MICK: Mick.

EMMA: Traffic, Mick, was not bad. Thank you for asking. *(beat)* I can guess from the chain saw that you're not here to prune trees.

MICK: No, ma'am.

EMMA: *(To Sonny.)* "Ma'am." A boy with manners. *(to Mick)* So how long's he got?

MICK: Actually, I was just about to get down to business.

EMMA: Well you can relax. Everybody can relax. I'm here, I'm a concerned parent, I have the money.

SONNY: *(Approaches.)* You have the money?!

(Emma pulls back.)

EMMA: Not so fast. *(Beat.)* Mick? *(Mick looks over at Emma.)* There's a cooler in my car. There's ice tea and some nice cheese cake. Why don't you cut yourself a slice and let me have a word with my son?

MICK: *(Hesitates.)* Jeez, I don't know…

EMMA: What's he going to do? Run out the door? If he runs out the door, shoot him.

MICK: I don't have a gun. *(Pause.)*

EMMA: Well here. *(Emma takes a small handgun from her beach bag.)* Use this. *(Mick hesitates, then takes the gun.)* It's small, but it can take down a moose.

SONNY: What the hell are you doing carrying a gun?!

EMMA: It's the 90s, Sonny. Everybody's packing.

MICK: *(Hesitates.)* That cheese cake. Is it ricotta?

EMMA: *(Smiles.)* There's another kind?

(Mick takes the gun and the chain saw.)

MICK: Ten minutes, Sonny. That's the best I can offer.

(Mick exits. Emma stares at Sonny.)

EMMA: *(After a moment.)* Well I can't say I'm shocked.

SONNY: Emma…

EMMA: What did you do? Borrow money and then gamble it away?

SONNY: If you have to know, I made a poorly calculated investment.

EMMA: What kind of investment?

SONNY: *(After a moment.)* Parrots.

EMMA: Parrots?

SONNY: From Brazil. *(Beat.)* And not just parrots, either. Medi-alert parrots. Parrots that could ride around on your shoulder and tell an ambulance crew exactly what's wrong if you pass out on the street. *(Pause.)* Problem is, they're very noisy birds, parrots. And when they're being smuggled into the country, you want to keep them quiet. *(Beat.)* So they were frozen. Packed into trucks and labeled as bio-hazardous waste. *(Beat.)* When we thawed them out they were talking, but only in Portuguese. I don't know what the fuck happened.

EMMA: Do you have to use that word? Mario Cuomo doesn't use that word.

SONNY: Mario Cuomo is not about to be split and quartered! Now do you have the money or not?!

EMMA: Not that simple, Sonny. You want the money, you're going to have to earn the money.

SONNY: And how do I do that?

EMMA: By treating your mother with the respect and admiration due her. *(Emma still holding the bag, walks around the room.)* You can start by explaining why you phoned everybody on God's green earth except me.

SONNY: Because I thought it would be a waste of time.

EMMA: Your own mother. A waste of time. How very, very nice.

SONNY: Emma...

EMMA: Not "Emma." "Mommy."

SONNY: *(Beat.)* What?

EMMA: It's a term of endearment, Sonny. Any woman who's forced a child out through an orifice not especially made for that purpose, appreciates hearing it.

SONNY: Hey, I never wanted to call you by your first name! You insisted on it!

EMMA: I never did.

SONNY: You said it made you feel younger!

EMMA: Well now I want "Mommy."

SONNY: *(Mock laugh, to himself.)* "Mommy."

EMMA: Very good. *(Emma reaches into her bag, takes out a bundled stack of cash, hands it to Sonny.)*

SONNY: What is this?

EMMA: It's a thousand dollars. I have eight more of those in here. *(Sonny stares at the money.)* See? All you have to do is make me happy.

SONNY: *(Looks up.)* How about if I call you "Mommy" eight more times?

EMMA: *(Shakes her head.)* No good. We need to progress.

SONNY: Where the hell did you get nine thousand dollars?

EMMA: I made it from the shop. It's been a very good summer.

SONNY: Bullshit. That stinking shop never turned a profit in its life.

EMMA: Maybe not while your father was alive. Because your father, God rest his soul, had the financial skills of a radish. I said to him when we went into business thirty-four years ago, I said, "What do we know about selling live bait?" He told me, "What's to know? You pay a penny for a worm, you sell it for two cents." That's the way his mind worked. That's why any other woman would probably thank God every night that he got drunk and swam naked into the propeller of that ship.

SONNY: You're trying to tell me you made nine-grand on worms?

EMMA: Not just worms, Sonny. I've expanded. I sell grubs, I sell minnows, I sell phony identification including driver's licenses and green cards...

SONNY: You do what?!

EMMA: Life gives me cabbage, I make coleslaw.

(Sonny puts the money on the dresser, begins making a drink.)

SONNY: I could easily overpower you and just take that money, you know.

EMMA: Well you should do that, then. You should walk over to your own mother and cold-cock her. That would be just splendid. A son beating up the woman who suckled him and wiped his "cooli." That would probably be something you could proudly carry for the rest of your apparently short life. *(Pause.)* What are you doing?

SONNY: What does it look like?

EMMA: Nothing for me, thank you. I'm on the wagon.

SONNY: *(Mock laughs.)* You?

EMMA: And what's that snide remark supposed to mean?

SONNY: Just that I never saw you turn down a drink in your life.

EMMA: Not true! *(Pause.)* I was a social drinker. I drank in order to mingle.

SONNY: You were a lush, Emma.

EMMA: It's "Mommy." And I now happen to be dry.

SONNY: Since when?

EMMA: Since seven months ago.

(Sonny has the drink himself.)

SONNY: *(Mock laugh.)* Emma on the wagon.

EMMA: "Mommy" on the wagon.

SONNY: Listen. Let's just save us both a lot of time. Lend me the rest of the money and I'll pay you back with interest in one month's time. Guaranteed.

EMMA: Like you can be trusted. *(Pause.)* You who all these years was too good to come down and visit. Maybe lend a hand in the shop. You who since he was 11 years old felt it was beneath him to touch a night crawler with his fingers.

SONNY: I've been an adult the past 27 years, Emma. I've had a life.

EMMA: Some life. You couldn't even stay married. To a good woman! An Irish woman. A woman who kept her mouth shut and could cook Italian.

SONNY: You never even knew her!

EMMA: What do you mean I didn't know her? We were best friends.

SONNY: You met her once, Emma! At my wedding! That was ten years ago! You were plotzed and the old man never even showed up!

EMMA: Baloney.

SONNY: On top of that, you kept calling her Angela!

EMMA: *(Beat.)* Because that was her name.

SONNY: *Her name was Kathleen!*

EMMA: Don't yell.

SONNY: And don't put it on me like it's my fault. Because it wasn't. We just…grew. We grew in separate ways. That's all. I was the one trying to hold us together, if you want the facts. She was the one who wanted to call it quits.

EMMA: Who could blame her? You were a lousy bookie who gambled away every illegal penny he made. You couldn't hold down an honest job to save your life. You were what women call a bum, Sonny. A leach. A parasite who happily attaches himself to the bowels of society. *(Pause.)* But I am not here to cast stones. I am here to do a mother's duty to her only child. It's up to you if you want to take advantage.

SONNY: *(After a moment.)* How?

EMMA: I'm glad you asked. *(Emma takes out a drawing pad and an 8-pack of crayons. She puts the pad on the desk.)* I want you to draw me a picture, Sonny.

SONNY: A what?

EMMA: A picture. *(Short pause.)* I doubt if you remember this. You were in kindergarten. All the kids drew pictures of their parents and brought them home. Except for you. You said you *did* draw one, but spilled your milk during snack break and needed something to blot with.

SONNY: I have no hint what you're talking about.

EMMA: Every mother on our street had a nice picture but me. I was alone in that my refrigerator stood bare. I now want that picture, Sonny.

SONNY: *(Beat.)* How much?

EMMA: Three-thousand dollars.

SONNY: Six.

EMMA: Four.

(Mick opens the door and sticks his head inside. His mouth is filled with cheese cake.)

MICK: Five more minutes, Sonny. That's it. I count to 300, then I'm in here zinging. *(Counts.)* One...two...three *(Mick withdraws.)*

SONNY: *(After a moment, to Emma.)* Give me the crayons. *(Emma does. Sonny goes to the desk, sits.)* What kind of picture you want?

EMMA: *(Smiles.)* A nice picture. *(Emma goes over to Sonny.)* The family. The three of us. And we're standing in front of a nice house. And the sun is out, and there are flowers, and a tree with a bird.

SONNY: We lived in a condemned apartment on Nostrand Avenue.

EMMA: Come on, Sonny. Create. You think Norman Rockwell actually had that much cuteness in his life?

SONNY: I can't do anything with you leaning over me like that!

EMMA: *(Starts away.)* Fine. I'll just call in the boy with the saw.

SONNY: I'm drawing! I'm drawing! *(Sonny draws.)*

EMMA: *(Approaches.)* Now. While we have this time together, I was wondering if I might ask you a few questions?

SONNY: Like what?

EMMA: Like how come you didn't make it to your father's funeral last year?

SONNY: I was busy.

EMMA: He was embalmed, Sonny. It wasn't as if he was going to use up a lot of your time.

SONNY: Come on, Emma. The man was a creep. He was worse to you than he was to me.

EMMA: *(Shrugs.)* That's not true. He was a wonderful man. He was very proud of you.

SONNY: Yeah, right.

EMMA: He took you to the Yankee game that time I was out of town.

SONNY: *(Stops drawing.)* He *left* me at the Yankee game! *(beat)* He sent me for a couple of franks, and when I got back his seat was empty. When I finally got home that night, he was playing cards with a bunch of his cronies. He looked up at me standing in the doorway and said, "God, that was quick."

EMMA: He had a rather off-beat sense of humor, your father. *(Emma smiles.)* I remember when we were first introduced at the CYO. I asked him his name. He told me, Lorne DeRee. I misunderstood. I said, "Laundry?" He said to me, he said, "Yeah. Laundry. It's a good, clean name." *(Emma laughs at this.)*

SONNY: His name was "Benito," Emma. Same as Mussolini. *(Beat.)* I'm glad he's dead. *(Beat.)* In fact, you know what I really get off on? I really get off on filling out paperwork that has that space for "Father's Occupation." I write "corpse," Emma. I get off on that.

EMMA: Never mind your father right now. Draw. *(Sonny sighs, returns to drawing. Emma peeks over Sonny's shoulder, smiles, indicates.)* Is that me? In the skirt?

SONNY: *(Looks at the drawing)* I suppose.

EMMA: Do me a favor. *(Emma picks up the orange crayon, hands it to Sonny.)* Make me a redhead. Like Lucy. *(Sonny hesitates, takes the crayon, begins to color. After a moment)* Sonny?

SONNY: What?

EMMA: May I divulge a little something?

SONNY: Give me the rest of that money and you can "divulge" anything you want.

EMMA: I just wish we would have been close enough so I could have told you some of the things mothers are supposed to tell sons. You know the kind of thing. Special secrets. The birds and the bees. Things a son and his mother—she being his first *real* girlfriend— should share.

SONNY: Forget it.

EMMA: A mother takes a special pride in knowing, for example, the first time her son...you know. With a girl?

SONNY: Emma, please.

EMMA: It's a beautiful thing, Sonny. Was for me. *(Sonny continues to draw.)* It was my wedding night. Your father, who was dashingly handsome at that time, picked me up and carried me into our motel suite at the Howard Johnson's/Sea Girt. Then he waited patiently while I changed into my what-they-called boudoir attire.

(Emma smiles.) And then he took me, Sonny. Like a gardener takes a beautiful flower. He pollinated me and treated me like the queen bee I was.

(Sonny looks over.)

SONNY: That's not the story I overheard.

EMMA: Oh, really.

SONNY: According to the old man, you spent the wedding night having your stomach pumped while he got a blow job from your Aunt Pearl with the goiter.

EMMA: That's not true!

SONNY: A real evening of magic.

EMMA: Yes! That's what it was! A real evening of magic! *(Pause. Emma smiles.)* Okay, now you tell me. *(Sonny looks up.)* About your first time.

SONNY: That's not gonna happen. *(Sonny returns to drawing.)*

EMMA: *(Slight smile.)* C'mon.

SONNY: *(After a moment.)* Why do you do this?

EMMA: *(Innocently.)* Do what?

SONNY: You know *exactly* what it was like. You were the one who set it up.

EMMA: I never did.

SONNY: Let me refresh your memory, Emma. My 18th birthday. You brought home a girl named Annie Eckelmann.

EMMA: That's right! I remember! I played Scrabble with her mother!

(Sonny stops drawing.)

SONNY: No. *(Beat.)* You *told* me you played Scrabble with her mother. *(Sonny draws.)* Actually, you never even met her mother. For all you knew, Annie Eckelmann could have been raised in the forest by timber wolves.

EMMA: She was a nice girl.

SONNY: She *was* a nice girl. I'll give you that. She was a girl with class. She was intelligent, she had a sense of humor, she listened to what I had to say…

EMMA: A veterinary assistant if memory serves me.

SONNY: I took her to the movies. *Born Free.* I figured, given her line of work, she'd like that. Turned out she hated it. She said later that she despised all animals. That she'd gone into veterinary work only for the free tranquilizers.

EMMA: *(Feigned amazement.)* No.

SONNY: Back at her apartment, she told me that she'd been transferred to a research center in Antarctica and was leaving first thing in the morning. That if we were going to make love, now was the time.

EMMA: *(Smiles.)* Isn't that romantic.

SONNY: Well, it would've been. Except that old Annie, who I think was feeling guilty at this point, admitted a few things.

EMMA: For example?

SONNY: For example, the fact that she was not a veterinary assistant at all, but a prostitute. That you and her had cooked up this whole little scheme.

EMMA: She told you this?

SONNY: Yes.

EMMA: *(After a moment.)* Sonny, understand. You were entering adulthood. You were a mess. You'd never even been on a date.

SONNY: So you got me a prostitute. *(Sonny continues to draw and color but with unnecessary pressure.)*

EMMA: You just said yourself. She was a nice girl.

SONNY: She was a prostitute!

EMMA: Doesn't mean you can't pick up where you left off. If she was a nice girl, that means she's a nice woman. Probably unattached. *(Beat.)* To be honest, I know this for a fact. Because we continue to stay in touch. She comes down to Wildwood to fish on her many frequent vacations. Asks about you.

SONNY: *(Interested.)* She does?

EMMA: Naturally, I couldn't tell her the truth.

SONNY: What did you say?

EMMA: I told her you were in the computer field.

SONNY: Emma, I can barely work a fucking pencil!
(Emma digs a slip of paper from her bag.)

EMMA: Look at this. I just happen to have her number right here. *(Emma leaves the slip of paper on the desk.)*

SONNY: I don't want her number! All I want is $9000 and for you to get the hell out of my life!
(Mick reenters.)

MICK: Time to rock 'n' roll.

SONNY: *(Approaches.)* Give me the money, Emma.

EMMA: After that? After "get the hell out of my life" you now want money?

SONNY: I didn't mean it.

EMMA: Not good enough.

SONNY: I take it back!

EMMA: *(To Mick.)* I'll be leaving now. It's been a pleasure meeting you.

SONNY: *I'm sorry…(Softly.)* Mommy.

(This stops Emma.)

EMMA: Mick. Sweetheart. We're almost done here. Do me one last favor. There's a case in the back of my car. Bring it in, would you?

(Mick sighs, nods, leaves. Emma picks up the drawing Sonny's been working on, studies it. She smiles.)

SONNY: *(After a moment.)* Is that what you want?

EMMA: Pretty much.

SONNY: Good. Now may I please have the money?

EMMA: I'm happy to. *(Beat.)* Now let's see. It's four-thousand for the drawing and another thousand for the intimate tête-a-tête. *(Emma takes out five bundled stacks, drops them on the bed.)*

SONNY: I need it all, Emma! The entire nine!

EMMA: You forgot to sign it. *(Pause.)* The drawing. It should say, "To Mommy" on the top and "Love Sonny" on the bottom.

SONNY: *(After a moment.)* And then I get the money?!

EMMA: Just about.

SONNY: What do you mean, "just about?"!

EMMA: One more little request. *(Pause.)* First sign your art work.

(Sonny goes to the desk, grabs a crayon, begins to write on the drawing. Mick enters carrying both a banjo case and his chain saw. Emma's gun is tucked inside his waistband.)

MICK: This it?

EMMA: Put it on the bed, sweetheart. *(Mick puts the banjo case on the bed, continues holding the chain saw. Sonny and Emma stare at one another for a moment. To Sonny.)* Go ahead.

SONNY: Go ahead?

EMMA: Play us something. That song we wrote together.

SONNY: Emma, c'mon! I haven't picked that thing up since I was a kid!

EMMA: *(To Mick.)* He took lessons for over six years. The whole time he lived in Wildwood.

MICK: Excuse me, Mrs. D. But I really need to get busy here.

(Emma goes to the bed, opens the case, takes out the banjo.)

EMMA: By the time he was 16, we threw out our television. Didn't need it anymore. We had Sonny.

MICK: Yeah, that's nice, but—

EMMA: His father and I could cuddle on the living room couch and

Sonny would prop one leg up on a wooden chair and play all night.

MICK: That's a wonderful story, but I—

SONNY: *(Approaches, to Emma.)* You know your problem? *(Beat.)* Most people have memories that work like a movie. No matter how many times you run it, it's the same thing over and over again. *(to Mick)* Not my mother. Her memory is like one of those things we had when we were kids. Where you write on this gray piece of plastic with a sharp stick and then pull it up to make everything disappear.

MICK: Etch-A-Sketch.

EMMA: Actually, I think he's referring to—

SONNY: I'm making a point if you don't mind! *(Sonny points to the banjo case. To Emma)* You want to know why I was never very good on that thing? Because you have to be *happy* in order to be good on that thing. "Happy" was an emotion I was not very familiar with, Emma.

EMMA: *(To Mick.)* This is my son being difficult. *(Emma hands Sonny the banjo.)* Here. Play.

SONNY: *(After a moment.)* If I do this, Emma, that's it.

EMMA: That's it. *(Emma moves the chair close to Sonny.)* Come on. The two of us. Like we used to.
(Mick sighs, sits on the edge of the bed. Sonny puts his foot up on the chair, picks a note or two.)

SONNY: Just don't expect much. *(A quick three-note intro. Sonny's not bad on this thing, but he's far from being a pro. The song itself is up beat, a real late-40s early-50s number.)*

EMMA: *(Sings.)* "There's no stronger bond
Than between mother and son…

SONNY: *(Sings, unenthusiastically.)* "We see it throughout history…

EMMA: *(Sings.)* "God may have helped Noah
Making plans for the ark
But who did Noah want
When he was scared of the dark.
There's no greater joy
Than 'tween a mom and a boy…

SONNY: *(Sings.)* "It's deeper than the deep blue sea…

EMMA: *(Sings.)* "Moses may have taught us
All about wrong and right.

But guess who Moses turned to
    When his money got tight…"
(And now Sonny's enthusiasm begins to increase.)

SONNY: *(Sings.)* "Bom, bom, bom…

EMMA: *(Sings.)* "There's no better tie
Than 'twixt a ma and her guy…

SONNY: *(Sings.)* "It's easier than A-B-C…

TOGETHER: *(Sings.)* "Even little Satan
    Had a mother, I note.
She wasn't very pretty,
    She had feet like a goat.
As hot as Hades got, she told him,
    'Put on a coat.'"
Because there's no greater joy…

SONNY: *(Sings.)* "There's no better tie…

TOGETHER: *(Sings.)* "There's no stronger bond
    Than between mother
And son.
(Sonny ends with a banjo flourish. Long pause.)

EMMA: *(To Mick.)* So there you go.

MICK: *(Impressed.)* Wow.
(Emma goes to the bed, picks up the money, puts it in the bag. Same with the thousand on the dresser. She hands Mick the bag.)

EMMA: Here. Nine thousand dollars. Count it.

MICK: *(Looking inside.)* I trust you, Mrs. D. If you say it's here, it's here. *(Mick peeks at his watch.)* You know, if I leave right now, I can probably still beat a lot of the 9-to-5 crowd.

EMMA: Just be careful out there. The inmates are running the asylum.
(Mick, with the beach bag, starts for the door. He stops. He looks over at Sonny and Emma.)

MICK: You know what? I'm not even going to go to Metallica. I'm going to drive up to Passaic, and see my own mother. I'm going to take her to dinner, and then I'm going to buy her some flowers, and then I'm going to tell her I forgive her for sticking me in the forehead with that fork. *(He takes the gun from his waistband and hands it to Emma.)* Here you go, Mrs. D. You don't want to forget your piece. *(Emma takes the gun. Pause. She and Mick embrace, then break. Mick starts for the door.)* Later, Sonny. *(Mick with his chain saw, exits.)*

EMMA: *(After a moment.)* Well, I suppose I should head out myself.
   (Sonny puts the banjo back inside its case.)

SONNY: You sure you don't want that drink?

EMMA: Want it? Of course I want it. I'm an alcoholic.

SONNY: Hey. I'm glad to see you finally admit something.

EMMA: *(After a moment.)* Sonny? *(No response.)* Was fun for a second there, wasn't it?

SONNY: I guess.

EMMA: We had a time or two, you and me. That's all I want you to say.

SONNY: *(Beat.)* We had a time or two.

EMMA: And your father. He was not that bad a man.

SONNY: Emma…

   (Emma goes to the bed, pitches the gun inside the banjo case, closes it.)

EMMA: At least he was capable of change. *(Sonny looks over.)* This being the truth, Sonny. This being my hand on the Bible and my foot in the grave. He didn't get drunk, he never swam into the propeller of any ship. *(Pause.)* It was right after his first heart attack. Right after he came home from the by-pass. I was sitting in the living room watching an old rerun of *Charlie's Angles,* when he comes out of the bedroom dressed in that cheap herringbone suit of his and says to me, he says, "Em, let's go do something." I say to him, I say, "Go back to bed, Lorne. They just split you open like a Thanksgiving goose." He says, "No." He says, "I just wrestled with death and I beat the son-of-a-bitch one-two-three. From now on I plan to live every day like it's my last. I plan to appreciate every second the good Lord gives me. Now go in and change into something nice and I'll take you out for coffee and maybe we'll ride the bumper cars." *(Sonny watches Emma.)* So I did. And he waited in the living room for me. And I put on my white dress with the buttons, the one that's just a little tight, and I put on my shoes, and by the time I got back out to the living room, he was dead. *(Pause.)* Just sitting there in his old Strato-Lounger with both hands on his crotch and his mouth wide open. *(Pause.)* And I recall thinking, this can't be happening. Not now. Not here. Not in the *living* room. *(Pause.)* The point is, he was capable of change.

SONNY: Come on, Emma. He was horrible.

EMMA: *(After a moment.)* This is your problem, Sonny. Nothing is horrible if you don't allow it to be. You got to pick and choose. You got to monkey with things. Put life in a dice cup, spill it out, and see what you get. *(Short pause.)* It doesn't have to be horrible, Sonny. Just the opposite. It can be this. *(Emma holds the drawing for Sonny to see. It's exactly what Emma ordered. Three people, clearly defined as two parents and a child, all holding hands. They stand in front of a house, next to a tree, and smile. The yellow crayon sun couldn't shine any brighter.)* Remember to take your vitamins. *(Emma exits. Sonny stands for a moment. Outside a car starts, then leaves. After a moment, Sonny goes to the desk. He notices the slip of paper Emma has left, picks it up, hesitates, dials the phone.)*

SONNY: *(Into phone.)* Annie Eckelmann? Sonny DeRee. From Wildwood. *(Beat, smiles.)* Yeah. *Born Free. (Beat.)* Listen, I was wondering if you might want to get together again. *(Beat.)* You would? Terrific. Tell you what. I'll call you later in the week and we can set something up. *(Short pause.)* Oh, and Annie? I think it's important that we get off on the right foot this time. Total honesty. You're what you are and I'm what I am. No bullshit. *(He listens.)* Yeah? Terrific. I'll call you. *(Sonny hangs up, hesitates, picks the phone back up, dials. Into phone.)* José? Sonny...Listen. On those parrots? What's the chance we pluck 'em, refreeze 'em, and maybe sell 'em as Cornish game hens? *(Sonny listens. The lights, along with his voice, begin to fade.)* Come on, man. Get with the program. Life gives you cabbage, you make coleslaw...

(The lights, along with Sonny's voice, fade to black. Curtain.)

END OF PLAY

Freud's House
by Laurence Klavan

BIOGRAPHY

Laurence Klavan's work has been seen on New York stages for many seasons. His work was represented this season by *Freud's House* in The Ensemble Studio Theatre Marathon and by *Miami Stories: Bellow, Malamud and Klavan* at the American Jewish Theater. His play *The Magic Act* premiered at Ensemble Studio Theatre and won the first annual Jonathan Sand Memorial Award for Best New Play. His short plays, including *Sleeping Beauty, Smoke, Uncle Lumpy Comes To Visit, The Show Must Go On, Gorgo's Mother, No Time,* and *If Walls Could Talk* have been produced by the Manhattan Punch Line, Working Theater, Actors Theatre of Louisville, People's Light & Theater Company, Philadelphia Festival Theatre for New Plays, among others. *The Magic Act* as well as three separate volumes of Laurence's short plays are published by Dramatists Play Service. He and composer Polly Pen received a National Endowment for the Arts grant for their musical, *Bed and Sofa,* which will be produced at the Vineyard Theatre in 1996.

He has written screenplays for TriStar Pictures and Warner Bros. and was recently part of the HBO New Writers Project.

His novel, *Mrs. White,* co-written under a pseudonym, won the Edgar Award from the Mystery Writers of America and was made into the film, *White of the Eye.*

AUTHOR'S NOTE

Freud's House is a comedy about a man and woman who use religion for their own ends. Both are sincere; both are right; both are at fault.

ORIGINAL PRODUCTION

Freud's House was first produced at The Ensemble Studio Theatre Marathon 1995. It was directed by Charles Karchmer (stage manager, Jill Paxton) with the following cast:

Sharon...Ann Talman
Eric...Scott Sherman

SETTING

A synagogue on the Upper West Side of Manhattan

TIME

The present. Saturday morning services over a period of time.

FREUD'S HOUSE

A synagogue on the upper West Side of Manhattan, during a Saturday morning service in the fall. Eric, in his 30s, shallow-seeming, his dark good looks starting to fade, sits in a pew. He tries but cannot control his laughter. Sharon, 30s, well-dressed, a bit ungainly, a prickly person, sits a row behind him. Whispering—disapprovingly—

SHARON: Shh. *(Beat.)* Shh. *(Beat.)* Shh!
  (Beat. The next week. Sharon now sits down beside Eric.)
SHARON: I can't believe it was you—
ERIC: Me, either.
SHARON: —who was laughing last week.
ERIC: Oh.
SHARON: I mean, I know you were nervous.
ERIC: I was stoned.
SHARON: Well. That's because you were nervous.
ERIC: That's a pretty snappy psychoanalysis.
SHARON: But it fits. Your first time in temple in years—
ERIC: In decades, forget a few funerals.
SHARON: Right. So you distanced yourself with a little dope—
ERIC: Or doobis, "as the kids say".
SHARON: And you got nothing from the experience, except that you
  showed up. Swell. *(Beat.)*
ERIC: Well, don't say it like that, Sharon. It's not nothing. I *did* show
  up. You don't know how many times I walked past that door and
  didn't dare—there's not a bookstore on Broadway for blocks, I had

to "browse" through the gum and candy in the drugstore next door, and you can't look inconspicuous doing that. So sue me if I needed a few toots on a fattie before I was calm enough to come in.

SHARON: You're not wearing a yarmulke. What would *that* require, a crack pipe?

ERIC: You're mocking me. When I really merit, well, you know, a Mazel Tov.

SHARON: Oh, that's a lovely use of the language.

ERIC: You're too merciless.

SHARON: *Can* one be *too* merciless? Anyway, about this subject, I don't think so.

ERIC: Look, I'll get to the headgear. Give me a minute. Or a month. Maybe. Jesus—I was hoping no one would notice, and what do I get, seen by somebody from high school, for Chrissake.

SHARON: Somebody. Is that all I was to you then? It's interesting.

ERIC: No. "Sharon Schaffer," I knew of you. I read the lit magazine you edited, what was it called, the—

SHARON: "The Long Island Epiphany."

ERIC: Right. I had no idea what that meant—

SHARON: You never looked it up?

ERIC: —until years later.

SHARON: You just went along, saying a word you didn't understand?

ERIC: Well—yes.

SHARON: Just like you did your Bar Mitzvah, reading the prayers phonetically, so you could get the party?

ERIC: How do *you* know? You weren't invited.

SHARON: I remember. *(Beat. Awkwardly—)*

ERIC: Well. It's really nice to see you again.

SHARON: Right. Look, it's none of my business, but just try to convulse *quietly* during the service this time, all right? And don't get picked up for possession in the temple, it could fuck up our fundraising. *(She rises, quickly.)*

ERIC: Wait, Sharon, where are you going, they're about to start the service—

(But she is gone, exits. Beat. The next week. He is waving her over.)

ERIC: Sharon! They're about to start the service!

(She enters, stops, surprised.)

SHARON: Well. You're back, one more time, I'm shocked.

ERIC: And don't worry, today I'm straight.

SHARON: On Rosh Hashanah, congratulations.

ERIC: *(Pats seat.)* Just—sit here.

SHARON: You're sure you're not saving it?

ERIC: No. My wife is shopping. She's—

SHARON: Even more serious about this than you are, I see.

ERIC: Well, no, it's not that. She's—

SHARON: I knew it. A shiksa. What is it with you boys? Fifty percent was the number in *The New York Times*. *(She sits. Beat.)*

ERIC: Please don't use that word.

SHARON: What?

ERIC: Shiksa. It's a slur.

SHARON: Oh, for God's sake—

ERIC: It is. Just because you're Jewish doesn't give you the right to—

SHARON: Look, if you feel this way, why do you keep coming back here? You take up space that could be used by the behinds of serious people. Are you just part of the yuppie trend back to church and temple I've read so much about?

ERIC: No. I'm not a yuppie. That means you have money and there's "upward mobility" involved. I'm part of that other percentile, the one that works part-time and has no health insurance. *(Beat.)*

SHARON: I'm surprised.

ERIC: Why, because in high school I seemed so—

SHARON: Insincere that I was sure you'd be a big success.

ERIC: Thanks. Well, you know, I'm not dead yet, I'm still just—

SHARON: Skating along the surface. I guess I should have guessed that instead.

ERIC: Look, I've been modeling, okay? I was even in a public service ad for the Army, on a local station in L.A. That's where I met my wife, Jodie, a lovely blonde who was an unlicensed acupuncturist. My wounds became infected, but we became close.

SHARON: Good for you.

ERIC: Well, what have *you* been doing?

SHARON: Dermatology. At Cornell Medical Center.

ERIC: Jesus, it's like a joke. And where's your doctor husband, he's—

SHARON: Not here.

ERIC: —he's at home with all the children?

SHARON: No, he's still…in my head. *(Beat.)*

ERIC: Oh. I see.

SHARON: Well, don't take *that* tone. I'm not dead, either. I'm still just—

ERIC: Waiting for Mr. *(Yiddish accent.)* Rright?

SHARON: So he has to be Jewish. I'm not ashamed of that. And I'll find him, never fear. I found *you*, didn't I, Eric, toking in a temple after twenty years? Miracles do happen. Maybe that's why you keep coming back.

ERIC: No. Actually, I don't know why I do.

(Beat. She sees he is sincere, softens.)

SHARON: Well, we're glad you do. We've been waiting for you, we who have been here all along. Have you ever gone to England, Eric? I went there two years ago, as an emotional mess who was in shrinkage three times a week. In London, I went to visit Freud's house, a tiny place he lived in at the end of his life, which for me was like Westminster Abbey. And there they showed some footage of his final birthday party, narrated in a strangely neutral tone by his daughter, Anna. In scratchy black-and-white, you saw this sunny day in this small backyard, and this sweet old man accepting gifts and touching little children's heads. But then his daughter informs us that Freud has just fled Vienna, and his sisters would be slaughtered in the concentration camps. Here he was, Mr. Mind, at the end of his illustrious life, and even he couldn't—in the end, even he had run from home, trailing blood, just an old Jew. Here he was, the inventor of the unconscious, stripped of psychoanalysis, reduced to just his religion—and I thought, if he couldn't hide in his head, what hope had I, who would never originate a thing? Everywhere I went that day, I was weeping. That's when I stopped therapy and showed up here, at my first service since high school. Maybe every time we think it's a psychological need, it's really a spiritual one. *(Beat.)*

ERIC: What is this, "we"? Since when are we "we"?

SHARON: Since the covenant. Or maybe just since the holocaust. And certainly since Pat Robertson and Farrakhan.

ERIC: I don't think so. My circumcision doesn't mean I now allow an entire people in my apartment. I think you might identify too much, at the expense of—

SHARON: My individual womanhood?

ERIC: Well, I would never be so bald as to say—

SHARON: But I bet that's what you're thinking. That the man who dropped me at the door—

ERIC: I didn't say a word about him—

SHARON: But I saw you see him—that what does it matter that he's a Wasp—

ERIC: How could I tell *that?*

SHARON: —that like everyone else, you're thinking, what's the difference, he's another doctor and he says he loves you, and how often does that occur on this awful Earth? You're too transparent, Eric.

ERIC: I just saw a suede collar and half a head of blonde hair. *(Beat.)*

SHARON: But in case you forget, according to Jewish law, as the mother, I would dictate the religious identity of the child, and that's a responsibility I don't take lightly.

ERIC: Apparently not. But, hey, don't worry, Sharon, you'll be fertile forever. Save it for your seventies, when you'll have some time. *(He laughs a bit, shakes his head. She looks at him.)*

SHARON: Well, what about you and your wife, where are all *your* black-haired, freckle-faced, spiritually confused, future cult member children?

ERIC: Well, I'm waiting, too, to—

SHARON: Typical—you can't even commit to something as simple as ruining the race—

ERIC: —to make sure it's the right thing for the two of us to do.
(Beat. She is surprised but hides it.)

SHARON: Right. You just say that because it's the holiday. *(Beat. Then they turn their attention out, to the starting service. Then—looking back—)*

SHARON: Happy New Year.

ERIC: Same to you.
(Beat. Another Saturday, a few weeks later. During the service. She is standing. He rushes in.)

ERIC: Hi.

SHARON: Hi.

ERIC: I'm starving, Sharon.

SHARON: I'm impressed.

ERIC: It's more than that, delirious—

SHARON: How many hours has it been?

ERIC: Since breakfast.

SHARON: So, not even ninety minutes.

ERIC: Right. But I'm—you don't know me. I have a child's metabolism—when I'm hungry, I get so cranky I could cry. And yet today I'm—

SHARON: Today you're—

ERIC: —so giddy, so receptive, like my head has grown into a geiger counter that goes off whenever it gets near gold. Everything today seems so—valuable.

SHARON: I don't think that's exactly the point.

ERIC: Of what?

SHARON: Of the fast. Of Yom Kipper. Call me crazy, but I think you're meant in a sense to suffer.

ERIC: But what if I can't? What if the more I try, the more—enthusiastic—I keep getting?

SHARON: I don't know. It might be—unprecedented. Don't you have *any* sins to atone for?

ERIC: Only that I haven't done this earlier. Not not eaten, but that I never—noticed. *(Stares at her head.)* Wow. That's a heavy-duty hairclip you've got on.

SHARON: *(Dryly.)* Thanks so much.

ERIC: In fact, your hair in general, the way it's, what would you call that style?

SHARON: "Put up"?

ERIC: Exactly. That says it. That says it all. It looks so—fetching. And *there's* a word I've never used before. It's amazing what you can find inside yourself when you clear everything out. By where lunch would be, who knows what expression I'll be using. *(Staring.)* To describe you, I mean. Sharon. *(Beat.)*

SHARON: Excuse me?

ERIC: I'm sinning. I'll have to atone for it next time.

SHARON: It's your stomach speaking. And I don't think this is the idea, either.

ERIC: I can't help it, Sharon. I'm going off. I've discovered you, buried beneath a jillion years of Jewish history. No matter how hard you pull it in over yourself, you're still alive. And still so—fetching. *(She turns away.)*

SHARON: Stop it. The Torah is coming.

ERIC: So what, I'll scream it—make it a sort of celebration. The most romantic high holy day in history.

SHARON: It's the religion you're responding to, not to me.

ERIC: You're both wrapped up together, you both seem to know what I need, you're both disturbing and inspiring, and I want you both.

My hunger is very—versatile. Maybe I know more of today's meanings than you imagine. *Yum* Kipper.

SHARON: Look, do Christians ever kid about Easter? Not about the Bunny, but about—or is it only we Jews who are so willing to make a mockery of—

ERIC: Don't hide behind this today. And don't shout at me, Sharon. I'm hungry and, as I told you, like a child, I...*(He bursts into tears. Awkwardly, she puts her arm around him.)*

SHARON: All right, all right...just relax...

ERIC: This is the most amazing day of my life...

SHARON: I'm sure.

ERIC: Your hands are so warm around me...

SHARON: Shh...

ERIC: Can't you be the river that I empty myself into, Sharon? Have I got the ritual right?

SHARON: Close enough. You stand on the shore and scatter crumbs to become clean. Except it's Rosh Hashanah.

ERIC: Oh.

SHARON: But I could be your body—of water, Eric. I could. *(Slowly, he looks up at her, astonished.)* I'm shocked that I just said that.

ERIC: Did you mean it?

SHARON: Maybe. I don't know. I'm so confused, suddenly.

ERIC: Well, I'm not at all now.

(Beat. They sit.)

SHARON: You see, he's asked me to marry him.

ERIC: Who?

SHARON: New York's only gentile doctor, my goy toy, my—shaygets.

ERIC: Wow. That word's even uglier when it isn't for women.

SHARON: That's not the point. Are you my way to say no to him now? I'm so nervous—how much could you have changed, Eric, since you were that beautiful boy who blew me off? I was always interested, you know, but you seemed across a continent in class.

ERIC: But being that boy has backfired on me now, Sharon. They say lines give a man character, but I've got lines leading nowhere. They're obvious to everyone, when I smile you can see them, I've been betrayed by my own buoyancy, my best thing. I woke up one morning and realized I had achieved glibness and that was all. How can I hand *that* down? I've been in and out of rehabs. In California, I was taking cocaine like crazy and Valium like a bored housewife waiting for her husband to come home. So was Jodie. Abusing prescription sedatives was the only thing my wife and I had in common. I came here because I've been—lost.

SHARON: I can't believe I'm learning this so late.

ERIC: Have you ever been to L.A.? There, you think Santa Monica and Wilshire Boulevards will always run parallel but, in fact, the whole time, Santa Monica has been bending and bending until, at last, the two meet at Trader Vic's in Beverly Hills. For twenty years, you and I have been the same way. Now we've crossed paths, Sharon— as if on purpose.

(She stares.)

SHARON: My God. You've come to me like some last-minute messenger in an old-fashioned play, to keep me from making this mistake.

ERIC: But I didn't know; how could I? It might be a miracle. Is that involved here today at all?

SHARON: Maybe—suddenly, I can't remember—it must.

(They stand again. He turns to the service.)

ERIC: Let me listen, and see what else I can learn.

SHARON: Someone should have refused to feed you twenty years ago, Eric. So much might have been different.

ERIC: It will be now. For both of us.

(He turns back to her. They kiss. Beat. Another service on another Saturday. Winter. They sit close together. Each holds a little wrapped gift from the other.)

ERIC: Why don't we open them?

SHARON: Let's save them until after the service. It'll give us something to look forward to.

ERIC: *(Smiles.)* If that's what you want.

SHARON: *(Whispers.)* I want to tongue-kiss you right here.

ERIC: *(Whispers.)* What are you doing?

SHARON: During the service, I want you to put your arm around me and then reach up under my clothes and completely cover my breast. No one will know.

ERIC: Sharon, we're surrounded on either side—

SHARON: It doesn't matter, Hanukkah's a major holiday, who cares if it comes around Christmas?

ERIC: Just wait a *little* while—

SHARON: I can't wait—I want you to slowly sneak your hand up underneath me and I'll sit on it and press down on it, and I promise you I'll come, okay?

ERIC: Even when you whisper, you're way too loud—

SHARON: *(Hums.)* On the seventh day of Hanukkah,
Da da da da da da.
Two Jews a-screwing…

ERIC: Since when do you make with the material?

SHARON: My God—"make with the"—it's a Jewish tone. I've taught you that.

ERIC: I always had in it in me—you just brought it out.

SHARON: *(Kissing him.)* I remember the first time I brought you out. I'd like to bring you out now.

ERIC: *(Whispers.)* Jesus, you're making me hard right here.

SHARON: If I could go back to that suburb in 1976, if I could tell that ugly girl spending her weekends writing pathetic prose, that this would happen, her hair might have relaxed, and everything might have changed for her. In the Hanukkah story, a little oil lasted an entire week. But my love has lasted twenty years. I'm the true Hanukkah miracle, Eric. *(They kiss, deeply.)* I want to see you more often. We're starring on Broadway in "Same Time, Next Yuntuv"— that's a joke, it means holiday—

ERIC: I know what it means, and it's more times than that.

SHARON: Whatever it is, it's not nearly enough. *(Beat.)*

ERIC: You know that I'm married.

SHARON: I know that you got married, I don't know that you are.

ERIC: But I am, I still am.

SHARON: What do you mean?

ERIC: Just that. *(Beat. She looks at him, confused.)*

SHARON: But you said you showed up at Shul because you were lost.

ERIC: And I was.

SHARON: But now you're not.

ERIC: Well, I'm working on getting where I—

SHARON: But isn't it because of *me* that you—

ERIC: It's all wrapped up together.

SHARON: It *is?*

ERIC: Yes. I can't just walk away from Jodie. I'd make all this a mockery if I did. Religion has taught me responsibility now. You've taught me it, Sharon.

SHARON: I have? Jesus Christ.

ERIC: You and Judaism both knew what I needed. You've both disturbed and inspired me, Sharon. That's a lot.

SHARON: But what about *me*, apart from the Chosen People? I have so much else to offer.

ERIC: Look, please don't drag this down to the level of "love."

SHARON: But isn't love above everything?

ERIC: I'm surprised at what you're saying. Coming from you, I'm confused, that word sounds so—small. *(Beat.)* I'm clean now, and type-setting for the Temple, but Jodie hasn't completed her hospital program. For the heroin.

SHARON: And when she does, what, your work will be done, and you'll walk down that lonesome road, like a hired gun for hopheads?

ERIC: Hey—hey—I don't care what holiday it is, you should stop with that shit, please. About us, the answer is no.

SHARON: My God. *(Beat. Then, more ferociously—)* Why isn't this just an excuse? Just more shallowness on your side? That you were never sincere? That you were just using me for your own...That you haven't changed since high school?

ERIC: Look, I've said what I can to convince you. *(Beat. She is pale.)* Let's open our gifts now.
(They do. She takes out...something in a frame.)

SHARON: It's a cover of my magazine.

ERIC: I found it in the corner of an old box.

SHARON: "The Epiphany." Was *this* what I was hoping would happen? Now it's just a brown idea behind glass. Poor pock-marked girl. *(Beat.)*

ERIC: My turn. *(He opens his. He takes out...a yarmulke.)*

SHARON: Last night, I thought it was time you put one on.

ERIC: So do I. *(He starts to put it on. She stops him.)*

SHARON: But now I don't...can't you—not? Not yet?

ERIC: But I should wait until when? The service is starting.
(She tries to touch him, but he has turned out. He puts the cap on. She turns out, also. She shuts her eyes. Beat. During a Saturday service, a few months later. Spring. Eric stands behind Sharon's pew. He wears his yarmulke. Her bag is on the seat beside her. They both hold "grogers," or noisemakers.)

ERIC: It's good to see you.

SHARON: Same here. It's been awhile. *(Beat. She is eating a kind of cookie.)*

ERIC: That's his hat.

SHARON: Right. "Hamentashen." Haman's hat.

ERIC: But what's the fruity filling? His brain?

SHARON: No. Only apricot. And it's delicious.

ERIC: And Haman was the Persian King's, like, High Commissioner?

SHARON: Yes. And "Purim" were the lots he cast to kill the Jews. But he couldn't.

ERIC: So that's why they hold Purim Parties?

SHARON: *(Nods.)* And you always dress up. As Haman, or as Esther—

ERIC: The Queen.

SHARON: *(Nods.)* Or as Mordecai.

ERIC: Who's her Uncle.

SHARON: And sometimes they give out prizes. When I was a kid, the winner was Barry Sugarman, who came dressed as a Unicef box. His head sticking out of a giant square with a slot in his side.

ERIC: Jesus.

SHARON: It's festive. A massacre was averted.

ERIC: It's always a massacre averted. Or a massacre.

SHARON: I think you've got it. *(Finishes eating.)* Oh, too bad, no more.

ERIC: Don't worry, I had breakfast, I'm fine.

SHARON: Sorry. I'm just so starved all the time now.

ERIC: Are you?

SHARON: Yes. But I guess that's normal.

ERIC: Right. *(Beat.)* Why? *(Beat.)*

SHARON: I'm pregnant.

    (Beat. He is shaken.)

ERIC: Are you?

SHARON: Yes.

ERIC: Con—gratulations. *(He sits.)*

SHARON: I'm sorry to spring it on you like this. But when do I ever see you otherwise?

ERIC: I understand. *(Beat.)* But—you are implying—you seem to say— are you so sure—it's—mine?

SHARON: Oh, yes. It is. And believe me. I wouldn't be keeping it if it weren't. *(Beat.)*

ERIC: Keeping it?

SHARON: Yes.

ERIC: Jesus Christ! *(Beat.)* I mean, okay, you know, I'm flattered, but—I thought we had agreed that—

SHARON: Oh, we have, agreed on everything. Don't worry.

ERIC: But—why not worry?

SHARON: Because—forget your own personal feelings, forget you and me, forget "we" when we weren't the bigger "we". All that doesn't matter any more. This is all about handing it down, this is about making sure it doesn't die. And that's all, Eric. *(Beat.)*

ERIC: Oh. I see.

SHARON: I promise you you won't be burdened. It's not bullshit. I have my own income. And no one will ever know.

ERIC: Oh. Well. It's not a burden then. It's a...blessing.

SHARON: And no one will ever know.

(He stands.)

ERIC: Well, you know, we'll see. We'll see about that. Maybe, one day, if everyone's mature enough to...

SHARON: Jodie is "everyone"? Who still doesn't come to temple?

ERIC: No, not yet. I've been trying to convince her to convert, but it's still...

SHARON: A hot potato? A bone of contention? I seem to still be focused on food.

ERIC: Up in the air.

SHARON: Oh.

ERIC: But I think it would really help her. I mean, why not try one more thing? *(He sits beside her.)* She's joined a coven now, that came from California. They meet every Monday in our apartment.

SHARON: Well. I guess you have your work cut out for you then. *(Beat.)*

ERIC: But—how about you? What would you tell whoever you—

SHARON: Esther.

ERIC: What? Who's she to tell?

SHARON: No. A name. For the baby. Because Esther was secretly Jewish.

ERIC: Oh. I see. It's like a reference. So, if it's a boy, it would be Mordecai, then, right?—if you were actually—

SHARON: You're right. But, anyway—Esther.

ERIC: —but naming a baby Mordecai, even if both parents *are* Jewish is really, in this day and age—I mean, you wouldn't want to—talk about a burden—and wouldn't that make—

SHARON: I'll, I'll deal with it.

ERIC: Right. Well, we'll have plenty of time.

SHARON: Right. Right.

(Beat. He looks at her bag.)

ERIC: Are you saving this seat? Does our bag belong here or are you saving this seat?

SHARON: *(Uncomfortably.)* The second thing.

ERIC: Is—someone else coming? Is someone else coming to sit beside you?

SHARON: Well, it's Purim, and he's never—

ERIC: "He"?

SHARON: Well, he'll be seeing his first service—

ERIC: "He"?

SHARON: —and so I thought—

ERIC: "He"? Who's "he" who's never seen a—

SHARON: You know, some men do still find me irresistible, Eric. *(Beat.)* Some—gentile men.
(Beat. It slowly dawns on him.)

ERIC: You mean…it's that—that—sandy-haired Wonder Bread bastard?

SHARON: Now wait just a minute—

ERIC: That piece of goyishe plastic surgeon shit?

SHARON: I think you're way out of line—

ERIC: That smegme-sprinkled mound of mayonnaise you call a man?

SHARON: He's circumcised, Eric.

ERIC: What? How do you…

SHARON: I just got engaged to him.

ERIC: You did?

SHARON: Yes.

ERIC: Jesus! Jesus Christ! *(Beat.)*

SHARON: I'd say I'm sorry, but it wouldn't be sincere.

ERIC: But how could you—how could you—you of all people—after all that you said…

SHARON: Suddenly, it didn't seem important any more, Eric. I mean, as long as I'm—continuing the…my conscience is clear. I can't live in a dream. Or always alone in life.

ERIC: But—but—but—it's mine. It's mine. Will he know that it's mine?

SHARON: Suddenly it's "yours" when we agreed to be the wider "We" in this. *(Beat.)* He'll never know.

ERIC: Well, what am I supposed to do? Never know how my own…Does *everything* hinge on hurt feelings? What is this, Sharon, purely to punish me? For a slight in Social Studies in the seventies? Or for my marriage, that I opted to—

SHARON: It's not that at all. You said so yourself, because of religion, you realize that you have—responsibilities. And so do I. I always have.

(Beat. He searches for an answer. Then—)

ERIC: You know, maybe you were wrong with your little story about Sigmund Freud. Maybe every time you think it's a spiritual need, it's really a psychological one. Maybe you've turned this into Freud's house, right here. And you'd do the same to St. Patrick's or the Russian Orthodox place on Park, where they always have the rug sales, or the Scientology building near the gay porno palace, or the…

SHARON: I don't believe that.

(Beat. Desperately—)

ERIC: But how can I always be apart from my own—my own—my own?

SHARON: You won't be. You'll be here.

ERIC: That's not the same thing!

(Beat. She looks back.)

SHARON: Here he comes now. *(She stands. He follows her.)*

ERIC: I'm going to say something.

SHARON: Please don't. The service is…*(She moves out past him, into the aisle, calls—)* Miles! It's me! This way! *(She stands there, looking back, waving. Then he looks front…and down.)*

(Beat. Another Saturday. A little over a year later. Sharon sits a row behind Eric. It is the Passover service. He stares out, stunned. He tries but cannot contain his tears. Sharon is holding, rocking, a baby. She seems serene.)

SHARON: Shh. *(Beat.)* Shh. *(Beat.)* Shh…

(Slow fade of lights.)

END OF PLAY

Credo
by Craig Lucas

Credo is dedicated to Robin Bartlett.

BIOGRAPHY

Craig Lucas is the author of *Missing Persons* (1995 Drama Desk nominee for Best Play), *Reckless, Blue Window, Three Postcards* (with composer/lyricist Craig Carnelia) and *Prelude to a Kiss*. Mr. Lucas has received the George and Elisabeth Marton Award, the L.A. Drama Critics Award, the Drama Logue Award, Guggenheim and Rockefeller Grants, the Outer Critics Circle Award and the Obie Award. *Prelude to a Kiss* received a Tony nomination for Best Play during the 1989–1990 season.

ORIGINAL PRODUCTION

Credo was first produced at The Ensemble Studio Theatre Marathon 1995, 18th Annual Festival of One-Act plays. It was directed by Kirsten Sanderson (stage manager, Tamlyn Freund) with the following cast:

Person ....Marcia Jean Kurtz

CREDO

Lights up. Person alone on stage.

PERSON: So it's Christmas eve,
I go out with the dog.
Jim and I have just broken up.
I've just been to an AA meeting
Where a woman got up
And said she had no friends,
Her best friend is her VCR
And it's broken.
I came home to the hole where the sofa was.
There's no Christmas tree either.
I can't stand the thought of sweeping up all the dead needles
And dragging the carcass out to the street
To join all the other dead trees
With what's happening to the rain forest.
I know the two aren't connected,
But anyway, I pull up a folding chair
And heat up a piece of cold pizza.
This, I think, is the low point.
The walls show little ghosts where the pictures once were.
I go out.

Did I tell you I didn't get my Christmas bonus?
Well, I wasn't expecting it,
But I haven't been able to take Apple to the vet about her problem,
So she dribbles a little across the lobby,
Past the doorman who isn't smiling at me;
I'm sure it's because I haven't given him *his* Christmas bonus,
But maybe's it's the trail of urine, too,
I don't stop to ask.
I smile bravely
And step outside where it has of course started to rain.
And people are running and looking very upset.
Surely the rain isn't that bad.
I turn:
There's been an accident on my corner.
I snap my head away,
I know if I look there'll be a baby carriage there
In the middle of the street.
I refuse to look.
They certainly don't need another person standing around, not
doing anything.
I put my mind…Where can I put my mind?
Vienna.
Where Jim has gone with the woman he left me for.
You can't escape these thoughts.
All I know is her name.
Her name…is Carmella.
Apparently.
And I believe that she has had a sex change.
As far as I know, this has no basis in fact,
But I believe it as firmly as I believe
That Bob Dole, Phil Gramm and Newt Gingrich
Are entirely responsible for the bombing in Oklahoma.
It's just an opinion, all right?

Where,
Where can I put my thoughts?
Ecuador.
My parents are in Ecuador.
They asked me to join them,

And I said
No, Jim and I would be spending the holiday together.
I hope that he and Carmella are caught
In the crossfire of some terrorist…
No, I don't.
Not really. But you know:
The sort of thing you see
On the evening news.
If you have a TV.
Or a phone.
Jim stopped paying the bills months ago,
As a kind of secret warning of what was to come.
But I refuse,
In my bones I refuse
To see myself as a victim.
I have gotten myself into this.
I allowed him to talk me into maintaining a joint bank account.
Everytime a little voice in my head would say
Watch out.
He's cute,
But he's not that nice.
Beneath it all,
Behind the charm,
His chin,
That first night,
And then again in Barbados,
Beneath it all
Is *him.*
I alone took each and every step
Which brought me here
To this street corner
In the rain
On Christmas eve
With my dog whose urinary infection
I cannot afford to fix.
And at that moment, my friends,
My dog squats,
And the worst thing that has ever happened to me
Unfolds before my very eyes.

A wire, a loose plug from somebody's Christmas decorations
Carelessly strung in front of their little tea shop…
Electrocutes my dog.
And she falls immediately dead
On the sidewalk
In a sputter of sparks…
And the lights go out all down the front of the tea shop.
And a man comes out:
"What did you do?"
And I drop to my knees, unafraid,
Let me die, too,
Electrocute me.
And I embrace my dog, Apple,
Whom I have had for sixteen years.
She is my oldest friend.
She has seen me in my darkest, most drunken days.
She has been to every corner of my life, watched me make love.
She growled at the dogs on the dogfood commercials.
She has been across the country and back.
Apple, I'm not afraid to say, is the purest,
Most uncomplicated expression of love I have ever known.
And she has been killed by an electric current
In the last sick days of her valiant existence.

The man stares at me from above.
"Oh my god" he says.
He can't believe it
Anymore than I can believe it.
Come in, he says.
We carry Apple into the shop.
To me she smells good,
But to some people she does not.
It's been too cold to bathe her.
It's hard for one person to hold her in the shower.
She doesn't like the water.

The man offers me the only thing he has.
Tea.
We talk,
And he assures me that the accident on the corner
Did *not* involve a child.
And no one was killed.

What to do now with Apple?
I can't cry anymore.
I have cried so much the last two weeks
I can't cry for her now.
And I know...
In some way I see all at once that
Jim was not really good enough for me,
That I will meet someone else.
And even if I don't I will have
An extraordinary and rich and complicated life.
It is entirely up to me.
I will most likely survive all the roadblocks and the detours.
As my dad always says:
"Life can be rough, but think about the alternative."

No.
I only hope that I will go as quickly as Apple
When the time comes.
And if I don't,
I will absolutely,
I *know* I will face that bravely
And with dignity.
I know.
And if,
For some unforeseen but totally justified reason,
I can't
And I am making a complete ass of myself,
Saying things I wouldn't ever say
And acting childishly
And turning into a prude
And a conservative
And am being a complete drag on everyone

For months and years,
I know my friends will forgive me.

And if for some equally valid and twisted,
But ultimately logical reason,
They don't,
Or they can't,
Or they're dead by then,
Or it's August and they're away,
Then I will forgive them,
Right?
The same way I forgave myself
For yelling at Apple the first time she peed
Before I realized what was going on.

And if…
Again, if I can't,
And everything is entirely for shit
And I can't even find my way to the end of a sentence…
And…you can fill in all the blanks…
That will be fine, too.

END OF PLAY

No One Will Be Immune

by David Mamet

    David Mamet is the author of many plays, including *Glengarry Glen Ross* (1984 Pulitzer Prize and New York Drama Critics Circle Award), *American Buffalo, Speed-the-Plow, A Life in the Theatre, Oleanna, The Water Engine, Edmond Lakeboat, The Woods, The Old Neighborhood, The Shawl, Sexual Perversity in Chicago,* and is currently represented off-Broadway by both *The Cryptogram* (1995 Obie Award for Best Play) and one of three one-acts that make up *Death Defying Acts.* Mr. Mamet's screenplays include: *The Postman Always Rings Twice, The Verdict, The Untouchables, House of Games, Things Change, Homicide,* and *Hoffa,* as well as an adaptation of Chekhov's *Uncle Vanya,* which has recently been made into the film *Vanya on 42nd Street.* Film directing credits include *Things Change* and *Homicide.* Mr. Mamet has taught acting at New York University, the University of Chicago, and Yale Drama School, as well as being a founding member of the Atlantic Theatre Company and Chicago's St. Nicholas Theatre.

ORIGINAL PRODUCTION
    No One Will Be Immune was first produced at The Ensemble Studio Theatre Marathon 1995 One-Act Play Festival. It was directed by Curt Dempster (stage manager Tamlyn Freund) with the following cast:

A..David Rasche
B ....Robert Joy

CHARACTERS
    A: a man.
    B: a man.

NO ONE WILL BE IMMUNE

Two men. A and B.

A: ...but when I saw the lights I thought I'd seen them before and I thought, "Yes. That's just...," then I couldn't think it was just *what*, because what could it be?

B: What could it have been?

A: It could have been...what could it have been? It could have been a...*car*. A car with a machine on top. A *police* car. An...*aid* car. Someone coming to aid. But it was not. It was *white* light. *White* light, do you know. Pure white, I remember thinking that it was not in the least yellow. Not in the least. And I thought that it could have been an *opening*, of some sort.

B: An opening?

A: Yes.

B: To do what?

A: To do what?

B: Yes.

A: To...to do what? *(Pause.)* To do what...? A *supermarket* opening. A...what did...?

B: ...yes.

A: What did you mean?

B: That's right.

A: You meant...you meant...I said an Opening, I meant Of a Store. Or something. But you mean An Opportunity.

B: That's what I thought you meant.

A: You thought that's what I meant.

B: Yes.

A: Or...I see, An Opportunity to do what, though? Or...an opening, it could be, an opening *into* something. Which is, yes, what we might mean if we say, and the word you used, was "opportunity." I often thought, if you could fill in the blanks. Of those things you misremembered, of those you forgot, as in a dream, or, do you see, a puzzle that you could not solve, the blanks, then you would have a story which, which, *another* story, do you see, which...

B: What are the blanks?

A: The blanks? Are those things which you...

B: No. What are the blanks *here?*

A: Here?

B: Yes.

A: In this. We have "Aid."

B: "Aid."

A: ...I could not remember.

B: ...what the *cars* were to do.

A: Yes.

B: "Aid."

A: And, "an opening." In *this* case, do you see, with lights. Scanning the sky. And why "a supermarket," rather than a *film?* Don't you think? *That's* mundane. "A Supermarket Opening."

B: ...could it have been another sort of shop?

A: What difference. "A Shop Opening." Its radius was too small.

B: What was? The light?

A: In the sweep it made. Yes.

B: It was sweeping the heavens.

A: "Sweeping the Heavens." How Sweet. Yes. But so it was. In this tight arc. In this tight arc of opening. Yes. Nothing escapes you. What a man you are. Sweeping the Heavens. A searchlight.

B: It formed a cone.

A: Did it?

B: You said it did.

A: Yes. It did.

B: Are you amending that?

A: I'm not amending it. No. "Then why did I hesitate?" It sees a violation. To me, and I say it's not your fault. Isn't that charming of me? But but, having it *reiterated.* In my words. You know? As if they were "set." It was ambiguous. To say the least. *Although* I chose the words. Yes. I said them.

B: You think that they don't do it justice.

A: Is that what I think? And I looked out the window. It was flashing. *Whipping* around. Slowly. It would form this arc. A circle. As it came close to my side, it would *whip* through it. And it formed a cone.

B: A narrow cone.

A: A narrow cone. All right.

B: Well, was it?

A: Yes. It was. All right. A narrow...any cone is narrow.

B: Is it?

A: At the point. You see: if one says *narrow*, that is only to describe the projected *height* of the cone.

B: ...is that so?

A: ...it seems to me. If we say *narrow*, then that is to say it seemed it was intended to rise, that the light was meant to travel over *distances. (Pause.)* You see. It could have been a helicopter. Landed, and shooting its beacon. That is to say, hovering, and playing its searchlight down. But it was not a helicopter. It was not a car. It was not a...a...and I broke out my shotgun. I loaded it. I started for the door. I started for the door. And I said "No." "I do not want to know. *(Pause.)* No. No." And I said to myself, "If you don't *go,* you will never know. What you saw." And I said, "Yes. I will never know. All right." And I stayed inside. I took out the shells. I put the shotgun up.

B: Did you look at the window?

A: No.

B: Why not?

A: I knew what was there. I fell asleep.

B: Did you think that was odd?

A: To fall asleep. When I was so...

B: Yes.

A: *Later (Pause.)* You see. I awoke. I half-woke. And the light was in the yard. The half-light.

B: In the yard.

A: Yes.

B: In the half-light.

A: In the half-light. Yes. I told you.

B: And it woke you up.

A: There was. It seemed to me. A flash. A flash. The same white, white light. Unnaturally white. As...*(Pause.)* as...almost...almost... *(Pause.)* I was frightened. Lord. I was so frightened.

B: Were you asleep? *(Pause.)*

A: I don't know. *(Pause.)* I don't know. I don't think so.

B: It was just outside your house.

A: Yes. *(Pause.)* Isn't that something? What can that have meant? What sort of man can that be, who is reduced to say, "Yes. They came for me..."? What sort of man must that be? *(Pause.)*

B: What is a "half-light?"

A: ...I...*(Pause.)*

B: You said "My God." And they reported that you said "my child."

A: ...it was all foreseen.

B: It all was? What was?

A: That, as if that were the magical phrase. It had the *power,* but it bore the *curse.* It had the *price,* you see? The moment that I uttered it, *before* I said it: how could I not know? Why did I *choose* it? And I wracked my mind for something *other* than...I said "my baby"...and I could not find it. Now: what can you think that means?

B: I don't know what it means.

A: It must mean something.

B: Must it?

A: What can it mean?

B: Tell me.

A: Tell you? That I, well, I, that I did not *want* to be forced to, forced...that it was *necessary*...*(Pause.)* That it was *necessary.* *(Pause.)* That, that, that, that...

B: Would you tell me, if you would, the exact words you used?

A: If I remember them.

B: Tell me the best you can. It's all right. *(Pause.)* It's all right.

A: ...but why do I find it so...

B: ...you find it...?

A: Because I could not find an alternative phrase. Because my *mind* ...my mind was...on the point of death. I had to *speak.* I had *to speak out.*

B: On the point of death. You said:

A: I've told you. But I'll tell you.

B: You said:

A: "Oh my God. My baby!"

B: And you told them…?

A: What did they report?

B: Please tell me what you told to them.

A: I told them…

B: Yes.

A: …that I had left my child.

B: You'd left it.

A: That, yes, that it was my…*not* my child. You see? I wouldn't, I couldn't have *said* my child.

B: You said your child *now.*

A: Now. Yes.

B: Why?

A: Because I *heard* it. You're the one who said it.

B: I said it.

A: *I* said "my baby."

B: And if you *had* said "your child?"

A: I couldn't have said it.

B: But if you had.

A: I'd have had to've…"corrected" it.

B: And how would you have done that?

A: I…

B: As if this were then.

A: I'd have said…I don't know.

B: Tell me.

A: That, that, I don't know, that this was my "day."

B: Your day.

A: I'd picked it up at *school,* I suppose.

B: …boy or girl…?

A: …and *taken* it…

B: …to?

A: I don't know. But, and why? I never told them.

B: You did not?

A: No.

B: Tell me now. In your mind.

A: In my mind.

B: Where had you left her?

A: In. It was. A...a *playground*. A...no, I've...what difference can it make?

B: I don't know. That's why I...

A: Something...something.

B: A girl?

A: What?

B: It was a girl you'd left?

A: I don't know.

B: What did you see when you said it?

A: I said "baby."

B: Yes. All right.

A: I said "baby."

B: Well. Say it now. What do you see?

A: A child?

B: Yes.

A: How old?

B: That's what I'm...

A: How old? Two.

B: Two years.

A: Yes.

B: Is a two-year-old at school?

A: Is it? I don't know. How would *I* know?

B: Think, now. Think, now.

A: I was speaking, I...

B: Think now, and tell me. Does...at what age does a child go to school?

A: At five.

B: Not earlier?

A: I think. Yes. To a nursery.

B: At two?

A: No.

B: That's too young.

A: Yes.

B: Where should it be?

A: With its mother.

B: And why wasn't it then?

A: It...it was my "day."

B: So, then, you would have taken it?

A: Yes.

B: From its mother.

A: Yes.

B: And took it where?

A: …to…

B: …to a playground.

A: To a playground? No.

B: No.

A: I know where I would have took it, but I don't want to say.

B: Why?

A: Because. Because. I don't like it because…

B: Yes?

A: It's *tawdry.*

B: Tawdry.

A: It's banal. What *can* this be in aid of? For not only did I never *say* it, but I have just demonstrated why, for *had* I said it, when it could not be unsaid, I'd be responsible, for *gaps,* for *knowledge,* which I could not know, which is why I did *not* say it. My *plan…*

B: It was a good plan.

A: It *was* a good plan. Yes. It *was* a good plan. "My baby." It was a *fine* plan.

B: And what are the criteria?

A: It *worked.*

B: It worked.

A: It got me off the plane. It saved my life.

B: It was a good plan, and it saved your life.

A: It forced them to turn back. You see? It forced them back. My mind raced. I had seconds. *Seconds.* And I had to think. What would convince them? What would allow me. To speak. To force them…

B: Were you frightened?

A: …to…of *course* I…*I* don't know. Of *course* I was frightened. And the only thought was: I had *seconds.* After which…*(Pause.)*

B: And then that was a good plan?

A: Should I have died?

B: And so they turned back.

A: They turned back.

B: You said, "Oh. My God. I've left my Baby."

A: That's right.

B: And then they turned back.

A: That's right.

B: What did the pilot say?

A: Ladies and Gentlemen, we have to return to the gate one moment, and...

B: Did he say he was experiencing Mechanical Difficulties?

A: How could he? I was screaming. In the aisle.

B: You were screaming?

A: They all *knew* why we turned back.

B: Why did you turn back?

A: To let me off.

B: To let you off.

A: Yes.

B: And so the plan worked?

A: Yes.

B: A good plan.

A: Yes.

B: As it let you live.

A: I think it was.

B: And what about the others. On the plane? *(Pause.)*

A: What about them?

B: Was it a good plan for them?

A: It wasn't a plan for them at all. *(Pause.)* It was a plan for me. Yes. All right. It was...do you see? I wasn't *sure*. I was sure enough to "divert" the plane, but I wasn't...

B: To "divert" the plane.

A: ...to...to...

B: You "weren't sure"...?

A: I couldn't stand the *ridicule*. How could I stand that? *If it flew.* You understand? *If it flew*...No. If It Did *Not* Fly...

B: All right.

A: No. If the plane had not flown. If I...how were they to know? If I'd spoken up. If I had spoken up, but the plane did *not* fly. How were they ever to know? *Tell* me that? N'brand me as a lunatic. If I'd stopped the plane. If I told them: This Plane Must Not Land. And, and then, nothing happened. I would have been..."This plane's going to explode"..."How do you know"...? *Beyond* a laughing-stock, and...

B: ...how did you know?

A: I told you.

B: Yes. *(Pause.)*

A: I saw the light.

B: You saw the white light.

A: Yes.

B: And you knew what it meant.

A: Yes.

B: What did it mean?

A: The Plane…

B: Yes. All right. Through what agency?

A: A…what would cause the explosion?

B: Yes.

A: I don't know.

B: Mmm.

A: A *bomb*. A…

B: Lightening?

A: No.

B: Collision?

A: No.

B: A Bomb?

A: Yes. I told you. Possibly. I don't know.

B: Did you want it to explode?

A: Did I *want* it to? *No. No.*

B: No?

A: What possible. No. What *possible* motive could I have…? How can you *say* that? How can you *say* that?

B: You said "What could I do. I could not tell them 'this plane must not land.' "

A: I *couldn't* tell them that. They would have thought me…*wait* a moment. *(Pause.)* Wait. *Wait* a moment. "This plane must not *fly*." *(Pause.) Wait* a moment. You're saying. That I could have said. What? Something, something. I could have said. Even *though* I was unsure. To protect the others.

B: I don't know. Could you?

A: What? To get them to…"cancel" the plane. Yes? What?

B: You got them to stop it long enough for *you* to get off.

A: I, I could have said something to get them to stop it altogether.

B: Perhaps?

A: What? I could have, what? I could have said, "There's a *bomb* on the plane."

B: How would you know that?

A: I, I, if I'd *put* it there.

B: Did you? *(Pause.)*

A: Well. You see. You see. You see. This is the problem. This is the problem. *You brand yourself for life.* What is a man's responsibility? Had I, if I had said, "I've put a bomb on the plane." How can you ask me to do that? And the plane *stops.* They *search* the plane. They find *nothing. Nothing.* They find nothing. I am sent to prison. Prison. For the rest of my life. Because I spoke up.

B: "You saw a light."

A: ...for the rest of my life. What am I to say? The plane. Returns to the Gate. They search. "I lied. I misspoke myself. It's *not* a bomb on the plane. I lied. I misspoke myself. I had a *Premonition...*"

B: You didn't say that you "had a premonition."

A: I said that I saw a light. When I saw it. I knew what it meant.

B: What did it...?

A: That the plane was going to crash. "And then you let those other people die..."I...*(Pause.)*

B: You had a premonition.

A: I saw the light. Had I not been on the plane, had I called. Had I called a *friend,* and said, "I've had this vision."

B: Then what?

A: They would know.

B: Who would know?

A: Everyone.

B: And they would know what?

A: I was right.

B: Yes. And the people on the plane?

A: I could have called the airport.

B: Yes.

A: And said. Ah. If I said "I've had a vision," would they have stopped it then?

B: I don't know.

A: Mmm.

B: What do you think you'd have had to say to stop it?

A: I don't know.

B: If you had seconds...?

A: "There's a bomb on the plane."

B: You saw the white light.

A: Yes.

B: You'd seen it before.

A: I told you.

B: Will you tell me again?

A: In the field.

B: Up in the Country?

A: Yes.

B: You thought that that light was…?

A: …something…something…

B: …that it had been a beacon.

A: A beacon, something, yes.

B: …to objects in the sky.

A: What could I think? What other use could it be? Shining?

B: What comes to your mind. When you think of it?

A: I don't know. I never saw that light before.

B: Just the two times.

A: Yes.

B: Shining. What comes to your mind?

A: A light.

B: A light.

A: A night light. I don't know. I don't know.

B: A night light.

A: …I don't know.

B: Who has a night light?

A: I just mean. At night. A light in the night.

B: You saw a night light.

A: To, yes, to light the way.

B: To light the way to where?

A: In the dark.

B: Yes. But to where?

A: *I* don't know. How should *I* know?

B: Who has a night light?

A: I…a *child,* certainly. A *child* uses it. Yes. I see it. I meant a *light,* do you see? In The Night. There was no child in it.

B: You said "my baby."

A: To get them to turn back.

B: Yes. Why did you say that?

A: Because it was so *precious,* you see? It was the most precious thing. That I could say. Do you see? At the moment. To…

B: You say in your fantasy, if you…

A: Why do you call it that?

B: Call it?

A: It isn't fantasy. It was…

B: "A plan." Beg your…

A: It was your question. It wasn't my plan, it was your question to me. Do you see? *(Pause.)*

B: All right.

A: It was never my fantasy.

B: Yes.

A: You ask me to imagine, and when I do, you ridicule me.

B: Yes. I'm sorry. You, if you *had* left the child.

A: But it *wasn't* a child.

B: Yes. I know that.

A: It *wasn't*…

B: Yes. Yes. Yes. It wasn't a child. It was a book.

A: No. It wasn't a book. It was a manuscript.

B: It was a manuscript.

A: Yes.

B: Of what?

A: Well. It wasn't real.

B: It was not.

A: No. I *told* you that.

B: It wasn't real.

A: No. It was…

B: This was your 'plan'.

A: Yes. "I've left my baby…Oh, my God. I've left my baby." that was all I said. There was no "child" in it. You've put that there.

B: I've asked you, if there *were* a child…

A: But there *was* no child.

B: And there was no book?

A: Yes. There was a book. There *was* no book, there was a manuscript. In my *plan*.

B: But it was not real.

A: The manuscript?

B: Yes.

A: It was in my *plan*. And then I told them. At the *gate*. This was my plan, you see, and why a child…"you had misunderstood. There is no child. I said 'my *baby*'…I have left My Baby…

B: And your baby was?

A: A book. My book. It's my "child." Do you see? My *manuscript*. Years of work.

B: But there was no manuscript.

A: I've told you that.

B: It was part of the plan.

A: To...yes. I would say "my baby," they would take me back. They'd say "how did you leave your baby?" And I'd say "I lay it down, and I forgot it." And they'd say, "Lay *it* down...?" And I'd say something, something, and it would come out it was a *book*. No. No. A book could be replaced. A *manuscript*. I had been working on for *years*. And what could they do? If I'd said "a child," they could... "check on it"...couldn't they...

B: Why...why...you wouldn't have left a child...

A: No.

B: Why not?

A: Who would leave a child?

B: Tell me.

A: Even a sick man would, don't you think? I would think, keep track of it. If it was a child.

B: If it were a child.

A: If it were theirs.

B: It would be a sick man to leave it.

A: Yes.

B: And who would leave a book he'd worked on. All those years?

A: It was an accident.

B: I understand. But if you *heard* that, what would you say?

A: People do it all the time.

B: They do?

A: I've heard of cases of it.

B: You have?

A: People leaving things.

B: Yes?

A: Precious things.

B: What?

A: Violins, mostly. *(Pause.)*

B: Is that it?

A: Famous violins. Stradivarii. Yes. *You've* heard that. People, lost in a cab, maestros, rushing, rushing about, and they've left, as I said, they left their violins in a cab, every *year* you hear cases.

B: And what do you think?

A: When you hear it? "The dumb fool." *(Pause.)*

B: What would the book have been about?

A: I don't know.

B: Can...

A: Just like an author. You see? With a manuscript. How should *I* know? 'Til it's done.

B: You saw it taking shape.

A: Well... *vaguely*...

B: Call it something now.

A: Yes?

B: Can you?

A: What I would say now?

B: Yes.

A: That it was about...

B: That's right.

A: "The..."

B: ...yes?

A: ..."Story Of My Life."

B: And you had left it. *(Pause.)*

A: It had been stolen.

B: Stolen.

A: Yes.

B: It's all the same. Isn't it? Lost or stolen; if you did not notice it. What would you say, of a man, who'd written, The Story of His Life, and allowed it...

A: Wait. Wait. There *was* no book. It was a *story*...

B: All right. In the Story. Let me ask you this. The book was stolen.

A: Yes.

B: Why would somebody steal it? As it had no value at all, but to you? Why would someone do that?

A: It was a senseless act.

B: But...

A: Wait, no. I, if they *asked* me, you see, I say "How would *I* know...?" *That's* all I have to say, *I* didn't steal it. Why should I arouse suspicions, by defending an act which is indefensible, no, the point is not that it's indefensible, but it's injurious to *me*...why did he steal it...? I. Don't Know.

B: Describe it.

A: Manuscript so-by-so, green, red corners.

B: It have a title?

A: I'd been working on it. But it had no title.

B: Nothing on the cover?

A: I don't want to say that, you see: if they *look* for it, if they *look* for it, then it might not "tally" with the thing they find.

B: They can find nothing, for it's not real. *(Pause.)* They'll *never* find it. *(Pause.)* You may describe it all you want.

A: I didn't have a title. I don't like to *rush* to it, before I know...you see? Before I really know...

B: And *what* was it about?

A: The story of my life.

B: You said if there were one place you would leave a child, you said one word, and it was "bank"...

A: Yes.

B: But where did you tell them that you'd left the book.

A: A hardware store.

B: A hardware store. What were you doing there?

A: I was not *in* the store.

B: I understand that. But *had* you been there...

A: ...why should I have been there?

B: Wouldn't they want to know why you'd been in the store?

A: But what could be more innocent?

B: More innocent than any other store?

A: No. Certainly not.

B: Then, if they'd said: "Why had you been there?"

A: I...

B: You can't say that you Wouldn't Want to Say...

A: No. Of course not. I needed batteries.

B: If they said Where Were Those Batteries...?

A: Ah. Yes. They must be someplace. Yes. I see.

B: You see?

A: I Put Them In My Flashlight.

B: If they said "where *is* this flashlight?"

A: I would say "in my home."

B: Do you have a flashlight in your home?

A: I...I must have.

B: Do you?

A: I don't know. I think so.

B: You see? For it has to be there.

A: Yes. I see. I *do* see that.

B: Then do you have one?

A: I *think* so.

B: You think so.

A: Yes.

B: For it it's not there, then they'll say "where *is* it?"

A: Yes. And it can't have "slipped" me, because I was just, I just bought the batteries.

B: Put yourself in the home. Put yourself there.

A: All right.

B: The lights go out. *(Pause.)* If the *lights* go out...

A: Yes.

B: What do you do?

A: Ah. I have this light in the closet. Yes. It's a flashlight. It plugs in. If the *electricity* goes out, it comes on. Automatically.

B: It does.

A: Yes. And you can *remove* it, you see?

B: Yes.

A: And use it as a light.

B: Yes.

A: You see...?

B: Yes.

A: You see?

B: Yes. A night light.

A: I don't understand.

B: The night light. It was in your closet.

A: I told you that.

B: Why was it in there?

A: To *shield* me. Should it go *dark*.

B: ...yes?

A: To *shield* me. *(Pause.)* Should...but, but, you see, I...*(Pause.)*

B: If it should go dark.

A: Yes.

B: You'd be frightened.

A: Yes.

B: But you said the *light* frightened you too.

A: What...yes. The light.

B: Because the light meant?

A: The plane was going to explode.

B: You said "crash."

A: I did?

B: Yes.

A: When?

B: Previously.

A: What's the difference?

B: Really.

A: I *meant* crash. The light frightened me. Yes.

B: Which light?

A: Which?

B: Yes.

A: In the Country.

B: In the Field.

A: Yes.

B: That light frightened you.

A: That's right.

B: I said A Light, and you told me that it meant the plane was going to
crash.

A: That's right.

B: The light that night in the *field*...it meant that?

A: No.

B: It meant *something*...

A: That's right.

B: That you said you didn't want to know.

A: No.

B: Why not?

A: I felt, I felt...

B: What did you feel?

A: No, you see, you see, I'll tell you: I...*(Pause.)* What I felt, was this:
that I did not want to attract their attention.

B: Yes...?

A: Isn't that awful?

B: Why?

A: It's unmanly.

B: It's...?

A: That I was *frightened* of them.

B: And what would they've done to you?

A: I don't know. How should I know?

B: Something.

A: Yes. Certainly.

B: Yes.

A: That's why. I didn't want their notice.

B: They would force you to *do* something.

A: Yes.

B: Should they come for you.

A: Yes. I said that.

B: And we don't know *what*.

A: What?

B: ...they would force you to do.

A: No.

B: But they came for you. They *did* come for you.

A: Did they?

B: After the light in the field. You saw.

A: I'm not sure.

B: You said you awoke. One moment. For a second. "And the light was in the yard."

A: I may have said that. But I'm not sure of that part.

B: But, you would say, that you *had* drawn their notice.

A: I don't know.

B: And felt that they were angry.

A: ...I...

B: If you had not drawn their notice, why did they come down from the field?

A: I don't know.

B: It must have been for *you*, must it not?

A: I don't know.

B: Why else could it have been?

A: I don't know.

B: Why else? *(Pause.)*

A: I don't know. Yes. It must have been for me.

B: Mustn't it?

A: Yes.

B: To force you to do what?

A: Who said it was to force me?

B: You did.

A: No. I didn't.

B: You said that if they came for you, it would be to force you to do something, "against your will."

A: What?

B: I don't know.

A: *I* don't know.

B: No. What *sort* of thing?

A: Something one would not do regularly.

B: Yes. And why you?

A: Why me?

B: Yes.

A: ...because, because...I've *told* you...

B: ...yes?

A: I'd *angered* them.

B: How had you done so?

A: By *spying*.

B: Spying.

A: Yes.

B: You were spying on them?

A: Yes.

B: How?

A: I saw them.

B: Doing what?

A: I don't know.

B: You don't know. Why?

A: Why? Because I was *sleepy*. I don't know. I couldn't *see* that far...I couldn't *see* it. It was a light.

B: Just a light.

A: Not just a light. This terrible...this terrible...

B: They came to punish you.

A: I don't know. I don't know. These are just feelings. Feelings. Do you know? I was so tired. I can't make them out. I can't make them out.

B: You said that you have no child.

A: No.

B: ...you...

A: ...you know that.

B: ...and that's why the book...

A: I said the book. Because I have no child.

B: So you could claim to have something.

A: Yes.

B: Something.

A: Yes.

B: To call you home.

A: To call me home. Yes.

B: Some reason.

A: Yes.

B: So you said "A book."

A: A, not a book, a manuscript.

B: But there was not a manuscript?

A: No. I invented it. Because I have no child. So I…my "Work"…

B: Your "work"…

A: …yes.

B: But you *have* no…

A: In my *fantasy*. You see? My *fantasy*. To Call Me Home.

B: To summon you.

A: Yes.

B: The light in the field. You said that you should not have looked.

A: Did I say that?

B: Isn't that why they wanted revenge?

A: …I don't know.

B: Because you looked.

A: I don't know.

B: If you had not looked, would they have punished you?

A: No.

B: …then…?

A: I didn't *want* to look.

B: …I know that.

A: …I…

B: When you had seen it, then it was too late.

A: Yes.

B: When you knew what it was.

A: It was, it was…how could you *not* look?

B: At the light in the field…you said the light was calling.

A: Yes.

B: Calling.

A: Summoning something.

B: "Summoning."

A: Yes.

B: As you were summoned home. *(Pause.)* From the plane.

A: The word's the same, yes.

B: Those on the plane…

A: Yes…?

B: People on the plane. Were they going?

A: …I…

B: Home. They were going home…?

A: They, many places.

B: Yet you said that they were going home.

A: All right.

B: You said that.

A: Not *all* of them, I don't think.

B: Those who were not…?

A: Well, *work*.

B: To work. Or to their home.

A: Yes.

B: To their wives.

A: Yes.

B: To children. To their *work*…

A: …I don't know…

B: If they were anxious to get there…wouldn't it seem…?

A: I don't know.

B: Why don't you?

A: I made the plan in a *moment*. I saw they were anxious. *I* would be. *I* would be. To be traveling. If I were going home. Wouldn't you be? To something *important*. You see? To their *children*. To work. Here I was, to interrupt their plans. I didn't want. To *anger* them. If I said…"There's a…" So I said *that thing*. To stop it. That I knew. That thing they could *respect*. That they could *understand*. I said "my baby."

B: And you didn't want to anger them.

A: No.

B: When you drew their notice?

A: Whom?

B: You said "a hardware store."

A: That's right.

B: You didn't want to say it.

A: No.

B: Why not?

A: I thought it stupid. I thought it banal. I thought: what a stupid place
   to tell them.

B: Yes?

A: That's right.

B: Yes? Then why did you think of it?

A: It just came to my mind.

B: Why?

A: *Why? I* don't know. I'd just *been* in one.

B: Yes? When?

A: Just the day before.

B: Yes? To buy what?

A: What? To buy the light. I told you.

B: To buy the light.

A: The light in the closet.

B: And why?

A: What?

B: Why did you buy the light?

A: What?

B: The light. *(Pause.)*

A: I was frightened. *(Pause.)*

B: Yes. You were frightened.

A: I *(Pause.)* I was frightened. To be alone.

B: You were?

A: Yes.

B: Since? *(Pause.)*

A: Since the Country?

B: Yes.

A: Since the…since the *incident.* Up in the Country.

B: Yes?

A: I. You know. It made me feel a child.

B: A child.

A: To sleep. With the door. With the door half-open. And the light. I
   was "frightened": is that so terrible? If it happens to *you*, you see,
   then you'd know. I was *frightened.* By what I *saw.*

B: What did you see?

A: I don't *remember.*

B: Where were you taking the plane to?

A: Back to the country. You knew that.

B: Why would you return there? If you were frightened?

A: Why? To *show* them.

B: ...to show them?

A: To make an effort. You see? To *show* them. To *conquer* them, do you see? To strike back.

B: You were angry.

A: Was I? Yes.

B: You said a beacon. *(Pause.)* You said it was a beacon. In the field.

A: What?

B: It was a beacon.

A: Yes.

B: *Summoning* someone.

A: Summoning them. Yes. That was all that I could think. It was calling them. Calling someone. It was summoning them to earth.

END OF PLAY

Dearborn Heights
by Cassandra Medley

This play is dedicated to
all of the Ladies of Anabelle Street in Southwest Detroit.

BIOGRAPHY

Plays include *Ms. Mae,* one of several individual sketches which comprise the Off-Broadway musical, *A...My Name is Alice,* which received the 1984 Outer Drama Critics Circle Award and is still currently touring regional theatres and Europe. Other plays include *Ma Rose, Waking Women, By The Still Waters,* and *Terrain,* all presented and produced throughout the U.S. For her screenplay *Ma Rose,* Cassandra was awarded the Walt Disney Screenwriting Fellowship in 1990. She is also the recipient of the 1986 New York Foundation for the Arts Grant and a New York State Council on the Arts Grant for 1987, was a 1989 finalist for the Susan Smith Blackburn Award in Playwriting, won the 1990 National Endowment for the Arts Grant in Playwriting, the 1995 New Professional Theatre Award and the 1995 Marilyn Simpson Award. She teaches playwriting at Sarah Lawrence College and Columbia University and has also served as guest artist at the University of Iowa Playwrights Workshop.

AUTHOR'S NOTE

Dearborn Heights is one in a planned series of short plays I am writing that concern the legacy of self-hatred within the African-American cultural context, the result of the long and enduring history of racial oppression in America. Americans of all ethnic backgrounds tend to want to either dismiss history or to invent a nostalgic, mythic, idealized past that never was. We love our heroes larger-than-life and without ambivalent weaknesses or flaws.

The two characters in *Dearborn Heights* represent what I believe are the complexities involved in "heroic" survival and endurance; complexities found within any group of people faced with contempt, bias, exclusion. The heart of the play occurred in a "burst of inspiration." A writer should only be so lucky at least once in her or his career.

ORIGINAL PRODUCTION

Dearborn Heights was first produced at The Ensemble Studio Theatre One-Act Play Marathon 1995 One-Act Festival. It was directed by Irving Vincent (stage manager, Gwen Arment) with the following cast:

Grace ....Linda Powell
Clare ....Cecelia Antoinette

CHARACTERS

GRACE: A very light-skinned African-American woman in her late 20s. She is thin and rather, "slight". She carries a studied "air" of self-conscious "refinement" and speaks with a soft, lilting Tennessee accent.

CLARE: Dark-skinned African-American woman, mid-30s. Rather hefty with a deliberate "commanding" bravado that disguises her vulnerability underneath.

TIME

A mid-summer day, 1951.

SETTING

A "homestyle" diner in Dearborn Heights, Michigan.

DEARBORN HEIGHTS

Grace is a very light-skinned Black Woman, late 20s, early 30s. She is dressed in the "dress up" style of the early 50s: A close-fitting hat banded around the top of her head, perhaps with a bit of a small veil attached. She wears summer net gloves, stockings with the seams down the back, 50s style high heels, a "smart summer suit" of the mass-produced variety based on "high fashion". Her pocketbook, which usually dangles from her wrist, is resting in her lap.

She is seated at a restaurant table. The table draped in checkered cloth, napkin dispenser, a tiny vase with a single plastic flower stem. It should give the feeling of a "homestyle" restaurant-diner. Several shopping bags and packages surround Grace underneath the table. She takes out a large, folded newspaper article from her purse, admires it.

The Andrews Sisters: "I'll Be Seeing You in Apple Blossom Time" plays in background, coming from an unseen juke box. Grace is clearly waiting for someone, she sips the lemon coke in front of her. A basket of fresh bread has been already placed before her. There is a second table setting with a second lemon coke placed across from Grace. She should appear to be glancing out of an imaginary window.

A few more beats and then suddenly her face lights up and she "waves" to someone unseen. She quickly folds her newspaper, returns it to her purse and waits.

Sound of a door chime jingling.

Enter Clare, dark-skinned Black woman, same age as Grace and dressed in the same style. Clare faces the audience. Grace waves as though through a window and gestures. Clare turns, crosses to the table with her shopping bags in tow.

CLARE: *(Fanning her perspiration.)* Whew! If it ain't hot as all-get out, out there!
(Smiling, Grace helps Clare with the packages which they tuck underneath their seats.)

GRACE: Oh you should feel "Knoxville" you think this is aggravating! I thought moving to Michigan was my release from "the fiery furnace", I see I was mistaken...truth is I done pulled off my shoes ha...I'm *(Whispering.)* "in my stocking feet".

CLARE: Ha. Well I'm 'bout to pull mine off right behind you girl...got a bunion that's "sounding off" like a bugle at the V-E Day parade!

GRACE: *(Gazing around.)* Ain't this a sweet place?

CLARE: *(Glancing around.)* Well...yeah...I guess...I mean why is it...well...empty

GRACE: Chile I come here everytime I come to Dearborn shopping...

CLARE: Oh?

GRACE: Copied their way of doing "tuna salad"...

CLARE: Where's the waitress hiding out? *(Looking around for a beat, she then smiles and gives a brief friendly nod to an unseen waitress in the distance.)* oh...good...

GRACE: *(Indicating the drinks on the table.)* See? Got us our lemon cokes

CLARE: *(Still staring out, puzzled.)* Y'see that?

GRACE: I been here couple times, trust me. I promise she won't be as slow as that salesgirl in the "Lingerie Department."

CLARE: *(Distracted.)* Ummm? Don't mind me girl I just...well when a place is empty makes me "jittery"...*(She "cackles" with a wave of her hand.)*...Starts me to wonder "what am I gonna be spending my money on"? Funny food or something...?
(Sound of a door chime jingling.)

GRACE: Ha...your turn to be the "stranger" and have me show "you" a new place!...see? here come a couple of people...

CLARE: Oh! wonderful! *(Settling into her seat, relaxing, buttering her bread.)* I am ready to "chow"—my stomach is about to "mutiny"...

GRACE: *(Pause.)* Well what happened? What did I miss?

CLARE: Humph! The "so and so" of ah Floor Manager finally decided to put in a appearance...

GRACE: *(Glancing at her watch.)* Girl I was wondering if I should have the waitress hold the table. I started to go back 'cross the street to check on you...wondered how long they'd keep you waiting.
(Clare stops and reaches down into her packages. She pulls out a box

and reveals a pair of long white evening gloves. She salutes Grace "army" style.)

CLARE: "Mission accomplished" under enemy fire

GRACE: *(Impressed.)* Well!

CLARE: I tole you if I waited there long enough and held out for that store manager…

GRACE: *(Overlapping.)* And they finally let you exchange them for the right fit.

CLARE: That's right! Boils me how they try and treat "us" when we shop in these suburbs…

GRACE: Well I'm impressed…

CLARE: They up there trying to tell me they "can't exchange my gloves cause they was purchased in the De-troit Montgomery Wards and not this here Dearborn Heights branch of Montgomery…

GRACE: *(Overlapping.)*…Wards

CLARE: Yeah you heard they "crap"! That's all it was! "Crap"

GRACE: *(Glancing at the menu)* …You gonna have fries or…you still on your diet…?

CLARE: *(Putting on one of the formal gloves as she speaks.)* I just explained to them with a smile on my face *(She illustrates "smile".)* that fine "I will make sure to write "The Chronicle", Michigan's largest Negro newspaper and to tell all my church members to make sure not to shop at Montgomery Wards period.

GRACE: That did it huh?

CLARE: And I tole, him I say, "You know Wards got no business putting better quality merchandise in the Dearborn stores then they got in the Detroit stores *anyway*"…like we "enjoy" driving out all this way into the suburbs just to get us decent…

GRACE: Well it's so "pretty" out this way…but no you right…you right…

CLARE: *(Pauses, shrugs.)* I guess they just figured, "Let's just get this colored B.I.T.C.H. out the way, what the hell"

GRACE: Nunno! no! what you did was…y'know…I admire…I mean… anything large or small that we do for the "Race"…

(Clare carefully packing the gloves back in their box, she then takes up her menu.)

CLARE: Dearborn is a very long way to come to shop if you don't drive…

GRACE: Is it? *(Pause.)*...Driving out here with you was nice but I like the bus...I don't mind...*(Stiffly smiling.)*
(The door chime sounds again as other unseen customers enter.)

CLARE: *(Smiling.)* Ha. *(Pause.)* That is one "sharp" hat you got...been meaning to tell you all morning...

GRACE: *(Touching her hat, smiling.)* Oh I collect hats, I love hats...thank you...you so sweet...didn't know if I should wear it just for shopping

CLARE: It's gorgeous on you girl! If you "got" it why not "flaunt it."

GRACE: People...well...don't want folks to think one is you know *(She makes a silent gesture to indicate "stuck on oneself".)*...people can think things you know...

CLARE: *(Placing her hand on top of Grace's hand.)* Girl...when that Moving Van pulled up and you and your husband got out...and next thing I know there you are out there putting in rosebushes along ya driveway, and I thought to myself, "thank you Jesus"... cause see we on our street are "vigilant"...the last thing we want is a bunch of "sorry", shiftless Colored Folk "ruining" what we all trying to build!

GRACE: Didn't mean for two months to go by 'fore I came over."

CLARE: You're a little on the "shy side" ain't ya.

GRACE: *(Smiles.)* My husband teases me...I thought you maybe thought...took it for granted I was...you know...*(She makes a gesture to indicate "stuck up".)*

CLARE: *(Smiling, waving off suggestion.)* Child pal-lease! Okay now the question is do I have the "BLT" dripping in mayo or...oh and "by the by"...they delivering me and O.Z's new television set tomorrow...Well ah right!

GRACE: *(pauses rather uncertain)* Well yeah...I think I'm gonna "miss" the radio...

CLARE: Now you can keep up with that crazy "Lucy" every week...

GRACE: Something well I dunno something "cultivated" bout the radio

CLARE: Child, last night, "Lucy" dyed her hair jet black, would you believe, and "Ricky" got hisself on this "quiz show" he had no business fooling with...oh they had me "in stitches" so I nearly choked to death!..."cultivated"...*(Pause.)* you got such a..."sweet" way with words I been admiring all morning how you...

GRACE: Some Negros get excellent educations down South contrary to what you might hear 'bout us!

CLARE: Course you gotta be "word-fancy" if you gonna qualify as "telephone operator" *(Graciously.)* Oh we must order something extra special, you're my first new girlfriend to celebrate!

(Grace offers a toast with her coke.)

CLARE: I'm living right next door to "one of the first five Negro women to be hired by the phone company", I tole my Momma 'bout it.

GRACE: Ah ain't you sweet! Ain't you the sweetest thing!

CLARE: Well the whole entire street is proud! my goodness! *(Pause.)* you make sure you preserve that pic-ture they had of you in the "Chronicle" for your children! *(pause, staring at her)* 'bout time some Negro women got hired to do something more worthwhile then that ole "mop and pail" stuff I be doing up at the Hospital! *(They toast with their lemon cokes. Pause.)* I tell you, here I am living right next door to a Negro Pioneer!

GRACE: Truth be told, when I went for the interview my hands were shaking so…I could barely hear my voice…

CLARE: Who cares? For the very first time in De-troit, whenever we call "Information" it could be one of five new Negro operators…could be you…don't worry…if I recognize your voice I won't "chat"…I know how to act as opposed to "some" of our people…

GRACE: *(Graciously).* Well now you got something to be proud of yourself now…standing up for yourself like that!…Whew that's what I luv bout being up North! Back down in Knoxville you wouldn't dare…they don't even allow us to try the clothes on, just have to take our chances…and you don't dare return it if it don't fit…

CLARE: Well I am proud to say I've never been "South" of Dayton Ohio where I'm from.

GRACE: *(Glancing over the menu.)* This being our first shopping trip together and a day of celebration…I say we "sin" and have hot fudge sundays…

(The door chime sounds again as other unseen customers enter.)

CLARE: Let's see the pic-ture

GRACE: Well…I dunno…I mean…

CLARE: Naw-naw…don't you carry it 'round with ya? I would, you couldn't stop me from showing it 'round if it was "me"…

GRACE: We don't want folks accusing me of the "sin of pride" now do we?

CLARE: So how's your hubby like driving for the Bus Company? Course my Clyde's got "lifetime" job security at Chryslers…

(Grace takes out a folded newsprint photo from her purse and hands it over to Clare. Clare reads from the paper)

CLARE: "July 23, 1952"...Course I have my "own" copy back at the house...

GRACE: Ain't you the sweetest thing! *(Pause.)*

CLARE: Some Colored folks might think I was causing too much of a "rucus" over a pair of gloves...

GRACE: Girl you don't know me! *(Laughing.)*...Wait till you get to know me better...I admire "spunk", "grit" as we call it back down home

CLARE: Well like you say...our very first "girls day out"...didn't wanna embarrass you

GRACE: The first of many! *(They toast.)*

CLARE: Folks keep staring at us Grace...don't look...

(Grace on reflex reaches her hand to her hat to make sure it's on right. Door chime sounds. Clare slowly gazes around. The door chime jingles as more "unseen" patrons enter. There is the soft sound of murmuring.)

CLARE: Act like nothing's wrong...

GRACE: What is wrong?

CLARE: Oh gawd...

GRACE: What?

CLARE: Oh mercy...

GRACE: What is it?

CLARE: Oh jesus, my jesus...don't stare! Sorry but...don't let 'em know we know...

GRACE: What? What do we know?

CLARE: Girl you made a mistake in coming to this place...

GRACE: You don't mean...

CLARE: That's right, that's the ticket alright...

GRACE: But...

CLARE: Everybody else is being served over there, over there...over there...

GRACE: But they served me! They always serve...

(Embarrassed pause between the two women.)

CLARE: Well! *(Pause.)* I guess they realize now that they "took a few things for granted" didn't they?

GRACE: Oh God...

CLARE: You had them "fooled"

GRACE: Gawd...

CLARE: Now they realize you...

GRACE: Don't "say" it...

CLARE: Ain't the shade they "assumed" you was...

GRACE: Jesus in Heaven...

CLARE: We better call on somebody...

GRACE: *(Mortified.)* Clare...I'm so...I'm so...

CLARE: Nunno...don't get up...don't let 'em think "we know"...

GRACE: 'Least down South they got...we got "signs" up...

CLARE: Well I never been down South, couldn't drag me down South

GRACE: I'm still not used to dealing with up "here"...the signals to go by...that waitress has always been so nice to me...how could I be so stupid...

CLARE: *Keep your seat*...keep your face in the menu for the time being...*(Pause.)*...We came here to have "lunch" and by-golly have lunch is what we gonna "have"!! They'll have to serve us or throw us out! *(Pause.)* Now then...*(Clare reaches into her bag and pulls out a ribboned broach the size of a small badge. She hands it to Grace.)*... "The Southwest Detroit Ladies Cavaliers" wants to welcome you as a new member!
(Grace distractedly waves off "broach".)

GRACE: Shouldn't we just get up and go...

CLARE: *(Reaching down.)* Don't look around...pretend nothing's wrong *(Smiling self-consciously.)*...now uh the "grapevine" tells me you being uh...shall we say "approached" by the "Metropolitan Ladies of Triumph"...

GRACE: Well...they have you know...uh...

CLARE: Oh I know they "after ya" right? They always scrounging 'round for "new blood" like "gnats at a picnic...not that I'm bragging but they ain't the Ladies Club for a Colored Woman of "quality"... believe me...

GRACE: Look why cause a whole lotta fuss? Let's just...

CLARE: Keep smiling so they don't know we're upset...hate it when Colored People don't know how to keep their dignity in public?...

GRACE: I am so so embarrassed! *(Pause.)* How do you tell up North where "we" can go and can't go?

CLARE: Grace you gotta learn the difference 'tween De-troit and the suburbs—Detroit and Dearborn, Dearborn and Detroit...me being President of Cavaliers means I can you know, "guide" you more easily then they can in "Ladies of "Triumph"...*(Pause.)* relax...lean back, let 'em know we ain't to be "budged" and we ain't to be "bothered"! Now then. *(Pause.)* Every year we "Cavaliers" happen to raise more than "Ladies of Triumph" do for the NAACP...why "they" was so "low-class" they held they "Annual Fashion Show" at the "Y"! "We" at least rent the Elks Lodge over on Livernois and 9 Mile...

GRACE: "Up North" was supposed to be so 'easy'...come to find out it's even more complicated...

CLARE: You just gotta fine-tune your sense of place! Look for other Negroes and if you don't sense 'em there then they don't want us there! Feel out the air around you!...We sponsor this "Gospel Jubillee" in the Spring that'll send you to Heaven and back...

GRACE: Down South it is clearly marked...please please pardon me...

CLARE: It is very unusual for any "newcomer" to get a "unanimous" vote from our membership.

GRACE: I shoulda sensed something...no wonder everybody's sitting so spread out away from this table...Lord the "cook" is peering out at us from the kitchen...!

CLARE: Let him...see when "we" shop in these here suburbs we gotta be armour plated inside girl...Don't let "them" push us around...! That's the spirit of a Lady in "Cavaliers"! *(Pause.)* Plus, as an added bonus...I'll teach you how to drive...guarantee you'll pass "the road test"...and don't you dare ask me to accept no fee! *(She guffaws softly.)*

GRACE: My man's the you know the basic "ole-fashioned" Southern type...he prefers to do the driving in our...

CLARE: Chile you up North now!! We the "new Negro" women up here!...*(Leaning in on her and softly poking her.)* I can tell ya want to...tell the truth...ain't you tempted by just a itty-bitty bit of independence?

GRACE: Thing of it is they know me here!...the waitress is "Mattie" over there...told me all 'bout her "bunions"...even promised me the recipe for "chicken-a-la-king"...

CLARE: "Mattie" huh? Ooough If I just had it "in" me to "lay her out" to her face!

GRACE: Clare please...

CLARE: I'm not blaming you—don't think that, you made a honest mistake...but see now this is the very reason why you need to join us "Cavaliers"

GRACE: *(Graciously smiling.)*...To tell the truth, very soon I'm gonna be

in need of the "restroom facilities"…oh otherwise I'd be all for sitting this out…*(Pause.)* 'Sides *(Smiling.)* I seriously doubt if I'm
gonna be able to you know, "receive" the proper "impression" of
Cavaliers—I don't think your Club Members want me to be fam-
ished in the process…

CLARE: …*(Pause.)* Ha. *(Pause.)* Sweetness *(Pause.)* Let us leave this
minute! Please—please pardon me!

GRACE: Nunno I'm the one got us into this…

CLARE: Nunno…"last" thing I want is for you to be put through…you
know…stress and strain and and "devil-made" conniptions cause of
"yours truly"…please…

GRACE: Nunno…it's "my" fault…but we'll just take our stomachs and
our business to where we can get respect *and* so we can concen-
trate…ha…

CLARE: Fine…All we need to do is just "maneuver" out of this here with
some lil bit of "dignity"…

GRACE: Just follow me to the door…

CLARE: Don't panic…worst thing is to panic…compose your face 'fore
you get up…

GRACE: Everybody's eyeing us…oh gawd…The longer we sit here it's
just more awful!

CLARE: I will not give them the "satisfaction" of seeing me panic…think
they gonna "run me out" oh naw! Get up when I'm good and
ready, "my time, not they time"…Grace control yourself!

GRACE: All their eyes trained on us!

CLARE: My dear just gimme one second…Don't come unstuck…you
are not "down South" now just keep a steady hand till I get my
shoes on…

GRACE: Fine…fine long as we don't get into no more monkey-business
foolishness, let's go.

CLARE: Wha kinda "business" excuse me?

GRACE: Clare…please…

CLARE: Please "explain" that last remark…calmly compose your face
and then we will rise and get out of here.

GRACE: *(Pause.)* There is no need for you to "order" me around in such
fashion…

CLARE: *(Taking a long gulp from her glass.)* Sons-of-bitches! *(To Grace.)*
Excuse me, pardon me.

GRACE: Nunno under the circumstances I'd say the same 'cept I got too much of the "church woman" in me...

(They pat each other's hands in mutual comfort.)

CLARE: I'll sit here as long as I can stand it—ain't gonna run me off like no "whipped mongrel"!

GRACE: Thing of it is they don't...they don't snarl at us or...or yell at us or attack in the same way they do down home...

CLARE: No I will not just "fold my tent" and like a lamb, "bleet" all the way home...Oh it gauls me...but they ain't gonna break me...!

GRACE: Pardon me but there is no need to make the situation any worse...

CLARE: I'm the "dark" one that's gotta get past their stares, walk through to that door over there!

GRACE: Now hold up Clare Henderson...just cause I'm light, don't mean I'm not feeling the same as you're feeling!

CLARE: *(Overlapping.)* Take it easy...Nobody's saying nothing 'bout your...

GRACE: Well what are you saying?

CLARE: Well who you calling a "monkey"?

GRACE: Now wait a minute here! We are not gonna lower ourselves to such a "level" now are we?

CLARE: Look if the "boot" fits then march in it!

GRACE: *(Pauses, then.)* Well! Trouble is "your kind" gets so...

CLARE: So?

GRACE: "Wound up."

CLARE: *(Folding her arms.)* Here we go! I knew you'd get to it sooner or later...the "darker" we come, the more we embarrass you huh?

GRACE: Look I'm the one they treated so nice "before"...

CLARE: Before me...

GRACE: Before!

CLARE: You wouldn't be treated like a leper "now" if I wasn't sitting up here, would ya!?

GRACE: You think it's easy? D'you think it's easy being taken for granted as "one thing" then facing the "flip" look when...

CLARE: Then you knew they was "taking it for granted" yet you lead me "in here!"

GRACE: *(Putting on her gloves, grabbing her packages to leave.)* I made an honest mistake. I'm "new" in this here city if you have the "decency" to recall.

CLARE: I got the "decency to recall" that soon as you and your high yella Clark Gable "wannabe" husband moved on the block, you've had your noses tipped in clouds, so high and mighty! *(Pause.)* Oh yeah anything to Lord yaselfs over the whole entire Street! The Block votes to get all new "look alike" Lamp Lighter Front Porch Lamps in front of each and every house...like in the white suburbs, but naw—naw! You and your husband gotta do something "fancier", something more "high tones"—just a tad one step above the rest.

GRACE: Humph!...Why don't you get yourself a "telescope" out of one of them Sears catalogues so you can keep your "busy-body" nose better in everybody's business? A neighbor can't "sneeze" and you report it to everyone!

CLARE: *(Pauses...studies Grace with contempt.)* And to think you had me "groveling"...at your feet to *(She snatches up the club brooch.)*...oh all them "begged" me to take you out, show you shopping...lunch you as "our treat"...but I tole 'em I said, "I wonder if she's not too siddity, too "high-toned" and stuck up for us."

GRACE: You are so damn "pushy" who would want to "join?" *(Grace reaches for her bags under the table.)*

CLARE: Damn you red-bone, "high yella", "lemon meringues." Always the first to be hired to the best jobs...always flaunting ya color, and every other Negro fawning over ya!

GRACE: That's right! "Vanilla" still beats out "chocolate" any day!

CLARE: Every night probably get down on ya damn knees and pray, "Thank you Jesus for making me light, bright and almost white." *(A pause, then,)*

GRACE: Is that what you would do in my place?
(Clare is stunned a little but struggles to hide it.)

CLARE: I tole the Cavaliers you had no intentions of joining us any-way...*(She starts putting on her gloves.)*...Or do you think it entirely "escapes" me that Ladies of Triumph all happen to be just about as "pale" as they can find 'em?
(Grace remains stock still.)

GRACE: Nobody's telling me I ain't a dedicated Negro woman same as you!

CLARE: Ha..."dedicated"!? *(Mocking Grace.)* "Lez Go, lez go 'fore we cause mo' trouble"...You can't wait to go "shuffling" out of here with your tail between you legs...*(Pause.)* so your lil "diner" friends have "let you down"…well "ta-ta"…*(Clare gestures dismissively to Grace.)*

GRACE: Hell with you, I'll sit as long as I want to!

CLARE: Fact is the rest of "us"…don't want y'all "high tone types…don't need ya…

GRACE: Oh you want us, you "crave" us…don't blame us if you faun all over us…

CLARE: Y'all don't have no real idea what real "color" feels like…

GRACE: And you do?…you and the way you and just had to "throw your weight around" in that store 'bout those "gloves"…not the principle of the thing I minded but you had to be so loud, so "pronounced" about it…

CLARE: I? I was "standing up for something? *(Gesturing with her gloved hand.)* but of course you got treated way way more "courteous" by the salesgal…guess you thought I didn't notice?

GRACE: I noticed that the other Colored shoppers were "cringing" but of course you thought you were "displaying" your courage in front of each and every damn body…

(Clare cooly lights a cigarette and studies Grace.)

CLARE: What's it like being "accepted" everywhere you go?

GRACE: And what the hell is that supposed to mean?

CLARE: Taken for "granted" as just a…you know…"normal" everyday "pretty woman"…what's it feel like?

GRACE: Don't you dare start "toying with me"…

CLARE: Since I'm so "bossy" and "nosey" I'm gonna be sure and tell the "whole block"…*(Clare pauses smiling with a sardonic expression on her face. Grace rises to leave.)*

GRACE: *(Mocking expression.)* You are such a "small-minded" woman.

CLARE: Why sure not as "sharp as you" girl. After all, as you say yourself, "They know you here" right? What's it been like? Lemme guess…here you ain't been in De-troit two months and ya already staked out a "nice" friendly "homestyle diner" in Dearborn Heights where you "treat" yourself to cool, restful, summer lunches… *(Pause.)* Tell me what's it been like Grace, so I can tell the whole street!

GRACE: No hold up…! It…has never been my intention that I was…

CLARE: What's that? Sorry I'm too "simple-minded"…

(Grace's face contorts in sudden shock and pain. She drops her head in silence. A long beat. Suddenly a tight smile crosses Grace's face.)

GRACE: Don't try and pull that outlandish crap on me.

CLARE: So she does her passing on a "shopping spree" to the suburbs, now don't that beat all!

GRACE: You the one who would want to wouldn't ya?…not me.

CLARE: How many afternoons do ya treat yaself to "make believing" you a white "heifer"?

GRACE: Wouldn't you just like to know…wouldn't you just like to be able to "dress yaself" in my dreams?!

CLARE: Thank God I was born with some real "paint" on my bones and not no poor "in-between"! Lease way's when folks "see" me they know what side of the fence I'm looking back from!

GRACE: "Fence"!? Oh and don't you just wish you could "open the gate!" Don't try and tell me you don't just—just *wish* you could scrub even just a "layer" of that "dirt color" down the drain…

CLARE: *(She is visibly trembling but softly taunting Grace.)* And we all know how ya got that "shade" of grey. Generations of "opening ya legs" for the wh—

GRACE: *(She is trembling.)* Don't care how much "face cream" and lipstick and "rouge" and…eye-shadow, and "Nu-nile" gloss on the nappy, hot-combed head, you still AIN'T gonna be *close* to being…

CLARE: *(Hurt but taunting.)* The real "true" woman you get to be everytime you "escape" …right? Right? And you thank God you can "escape" …don't cha! Don't cha!

GRACE: *(Nodding.)* Absolutely…Abso…*(Realizing what she's saying, she cringes, drops her head.)*
(Suddenly there is a ground swell of sound. The unseen white patrons begin banging tableware against glassware to protest Grace and Clare's presence. They both look up startled.)

CLARE: *(Softly, grabbing Grace's hand.)* Don't turn around Grace…don't let 'em see your fear…

GRACE: But what if they…if they grab us…if they punch us…

CLARE: They too "gen-teel" for that…we're just "women" and it's just two of us…they won't go too far…*(Clare lifts her glass and shouts outloud, facing the audience)* Well I got a lemoncoke out of it, nothing you can do about that can ya!! Smash the glass but you can't take the coke back!!

UNSEEN VOICE: Get on back to De-troit where you niggers belong!
(Grace takes a long sweeping look at the audience, she stares at Clare as they gather their packages.)

GRACE: Oh it "gauls me"...oh it "gauls me"

CLARE: *(Softly smiling.)* Welcome to the "Motor Capital of the World" *(They rise together. They stare out at the audience as they clutch each other's arms and hold their heads high. They take slow steps toward the audience. Soft "cackling" from an unseen "crowd" can be heard in background. They take slow "dignified" steps towards audience. They "cross" a lighted boundary, the door chime "sounds", traffic noise, they are standing face front to the audience with the impression that they are now outside the Diner. They still clutch each other for a few moments, then pull away.)*

CLARE: *(Panting.)* Feels like I'm a icicle all over

GRACE: My heart's racing...racing...

CLARE: Lemme just stop shaking...ha...

GRACE: My heart's pounding...

(Suddenly Clare checks her packages.)

CLARE: Did we get everything Grace...*(Quickly counting her packages, pause, frantically.)* whew!...we made it...ha...one day we'll tell our kids how we stood up to the crackers one summer day in Dearborn Heights!

(It is obvious they are too embarrassed to look each other in the face.)

GRACE: *(Pause, then.)* To think all that ugly could come out of my mouth...

CLARE: All that trash I was talking...please...don't see how you could ever "pardon" me...

(Clare tries to answer, cannot. Softly.)

CLARE: Did have all the Colored cringing back at Montgomery Wards?

GRACE: *(Turning to her.)* Nunno...you stood up for...

CLARE: *(Overlapping.)*...No you were right...I embarrassed everybody...

GRACE: Colored Rights!

CLARE: I was so...so loud and bodacious...tell me true now...

GRACE: What could I say to you that you could possibly believe after today? *(Staring out in a daze.)* They...they...got to see the..."base" side of us that's what gets to me.

CLARE: *(Pause.)* You left me standing there at the counter, I must have been behaving pretty awful.

GRACE: *(Pause.)* Clare, *(Pause.)* understand something...I may have "crossed" the Mason-Dixon line but it's still in me...Even when I take the long ride out here on the bus just to go past all the lovely homes and gardens? Still can't bring myself to take a seat sit "up front" even though I know we're "allowed" to up North here…and I can't even tell my husband that.

(They both smile to each other a moment.)

CLARE: Know what we need? *(Pause.)* We need ta "shop" all this out our system…calm our nerves…ha ha…okay Hudson's here we come…gonna get me some new patent-leather heels right now! Where'd I park m'car? I'm so frazzled.

(Clare begins to move off, Grace stops her with her voice.)

GRACE: First time I went there I really didn't "think" of it as "passing"… *(Pause.)* but then again, didn't I? And then the next time…and then the next…

CLARE: Don't start "unraveling" nothing!…Leave where it lays, forget it took place, come on…

GRACE: but…truth be told…when I really deep down think about it

CLARE: *(Smiling.)* Oh to hell with the "truth"…thinking too much frays the nerves, don't you know that…

GRACE: Clare…! *(Pause.)* Everytime we meet up "today" is gonna be "behind" our eyes, our…smiles…our "hellos" *(Grace grabs Clare's hand for a moment as they still look away. Embarrassed Clare pats Grace's hand, gently pulls off and "brightens".)*

CLARE: Now we gonna get the car, get back cross the line to De-troit and get us some food in us 'fore we faint from this heat…

GRACE: Will I tell O.Z. about today I wonder? Will you tell Clyde?

CLARE: I always say it's a wise woman who charts a clear course 'tween women's business and men's.

GRACE: Now if I join up with Cavaliers you'll probably think…

CLARE: No I will not…

GRACE: I'm feeling obliged in some way…

CLARE: No you mistake…*I don't intend to "think" about it ever*…*(Pause.)* I guess I "push against" folks…so I don't Break me…*(Pause, studies Grace, then.)*…I say we "toss" this whole day in the pile marked, "never happened" and stop feeding on it, period…

GRACE: It's not just gonna dissolve away…

CLARE: Don't fool yaself…pieces fall away bit by bit till finally it's just a haze of a recollection way, way back…then presto, it never happened.

GRACE: *(Pause.)* Wonder if one day we might end up "real buddies"…

CLARE: *(Pause. Smiling.)* Could be dangerous to your home life. *(Pause,* smiles.)...For one thing, you just might end up learning how to drive.

GRACE: *(Giggling.)* Ha. *(Then she suddenly turns somber.)*... "Toss it back and forget it ever happened..."?

(Pause. They stare off in different directions. Grace removes her sunglasses from her purse, puts them on. Clare takes out her compact, check's her face.)

CLARE: *(Her face is a smiling "mask".)* I already have...

GRACE: *(Pause, then.)* "Dearborn Heights."

(Fade out.)

END OF PLAY

The Ryan Interview,
Or How It Was Around Here
by Arthur Miller

BIOGRAPHY

Arthur Miller was born in New York City in 1915. He went to the University of Michigan, where two plays were produced in 1934. When he graduated in 1938, he began work with the Federal Theatre Project. His first Broadway production was *The Man Who Had All the Luck* ; his next play, *All My Sons,* won the Drama Critics' Circle award. In 1949, Mr. Miller's *Death of a Salesman* was given the Pulitzer Prize and the Drama Critics' Circle Award. *The Crucible* won a Tony Award four years later. *A View From the Bridge, A Memory of Two Mondays, The Price, After the Fall, Incident at Vichy , The American Clock, The Archbishop's Ceiling,* a novel, stories and essays are among his other works. *Timebends,* his autobiography, was published in 1987.

His screenplays include *The Misfits* and the play for television, *Playing For Time.* His original screenplay *Everybody Wins* was directed by Karel Reisz and starred Debra Winger and Nick Nolte (released January 1990 in the United States). Two books of reportage, *In Russia* and *Chinese Encounters* were accompanied by photographs by his wife, the famed Inge Morath. His book, *Salesman in Beijing,* is based on his experience in China, where he directed *Death of A Salesman.* Recent productions of his plays include *A View From The Bridge* and *Death of a Salesman* starring Dustin Hoffman on Broadway, *Up From Paradise* and *After the Fall* off-Broadway and two one-act plays called *Elegy For A Lady* and *Some Kind of Love Story (Two Way Mirror)* at the Young Vic in London as well as revival of *An Enemy of the People* which transferred from the Young Vic to the Playhouse Theatre in London. The Young Vic in London did *The Price* in February 1990. At the National Theatre in London were productions of *The Crucible* and *After the Fall.*

His play *The Ride Down Mt. Morgan* opened in London in October 1991, directed by Michael Blakemore, starring Tom Conti. *The Last Yankee* opened January 5, 1993 at Manhattan Theatre Club in New York City, and at the Young Vic in London on January 26, 1993, directed by David Thacker, and transferred to the West End on April 27, 1993. His newest play *Broken Glass,* opened at the Long Wharf Theatre in New Haven, Connecticut on March 1, 1994. It opened at the Booth Theatre on Broadway on April 24, 1994 and opened at the National Theatre in London August 1994. It transferred to the West End in February 1995 where it won the Olivier Award for Best Play in April 1995 and is now on tour. Also, *A View From The Bridge* transferred to the West End in April 1995.

The Film version of *The Crucible* to be produced by Fox will be directed by Nicholas Hytner and will star Daniel Day Lewis, Winona Ryder, Paul Scofield and will begin production in September 1995.

AUTHOR'S NOTE

Here and there in the American countryside are still a few people with memories of a different time entirely, when—in a word—porches still had people on them talking across railings from house to house rather than crouching in the dark peering at the screen. There is another country in these old guys' heads, one they can't return to or quite leave behind.

ORIGINAL PRODUCTION

The Ryan Interview was first produced at The Ensemble Studio Theatre One-Act Play Marathon 1995, 18th Annual Festival of one-act plays. It was directed by Curt Dempster (assistant director, Anna Basoli) with the following cast:

Interviewer ....Julie Lauren
Ryan..Mason Adams

SETTING

The porch of a small house in the country.

THE RYAN INTERVIEW, OR HOW IT WAS AROUND HERE

The reporter, a woman, is seated in an old chair on Ryan's front porch. Ryan enters from inside the house and hands her a cup of water.

RYAN: Here you are.

REPORTER: Thank you.

RYAN: Yes ma'am. *(Sits in his chair.)*

REPORTER: I'd like to thank you for agreeing to talk to me, Mr. Ryan.

RYAN: I never mind talking, what'd you want to ask me? I didn't know they had women doing this.

REPORTER: Oh, there are lots of us, yes. Do you mind?

RYAN: No, I don't mind.—I worked down a lot of basements but never inside the house. That's women's work. But I guess that's all changed by now.—Go ahead, I'm not due anywhere. This is my hundredth birthday, you know.

REPORTER: Gonna have a party?

RYAN: Oh, no. They're all dead and gone.

REPORTER: A hundredth birthday is a very special occasion that's why we wrote you a letter about an interview.

RYAN: I guess I have it on my bureau. Is this going to be in the paper?

REPORTER: Oh, yes. Would you mind if I tape-recorded this?

RYAN: Well…I guess it won't do any harm. I lost my glasses but I'll read the letter some other time.

REPORTER: I'll just put it right here as a backup. *(She sets the tape recorder on a crate in front of him.)*

RYAN: You're probably surprised that I'm a hundred.

REPORTER: You certainly don't look it.

RYAN: I got stuck at sixty and never looked a day older. When I was seventy they thought I was sixty. When I was eighty and ninety they still took me for sixty. But I sure feel like I'm a hundred. You got any idea what it feels like to be a hundred?

REPORTER: That's one of the things I wanted to ask you.

RYAN: Well, there's nothing like it. Not even ninety-nine.

REPORTER: Well could you describe it?

RYAN: Well, let's see. *(Pause.)* No, I don't guess I could.—You can ask me more if you like, I'm not due anywhere.

REPORTER: You were never married I understand.

RYAN: Never met anybody who'd have me.

REPORTER: Why not? Even now you're a good-looking man.

RYAN: I was always good-looking, but to tell you the truth, women mostly made me nervous.

REPORTER: Really. Have you any idea why?

RYAN: Well, let's see. *(Pause.)* Nope.

REPORTER: But there must be some reason.

RYAN: I always thought they was peculiar.

REPORTER: In what way?

RYAN: Oh, I don't know—the usual way. How about you?

REPORTER: What do you mean?

RYAN: You married?

REPORTER: Well, not really. I mean no, I'm not. I mean, I was until a few months ago. So I'm still not used to saying that I'm not married I mean.

RYAN: I didn't mean to—

REPORTER: No, no that's okay.—So then you lived alone your whole life?

RYAN: Well…I guess so, but they was always a lot of people around that…I mean it wasn't like I was alone, don't you know.

REPORTER: Yes, I see. Could I ask you about the area? This was mostly farmland, wasn't it.

RYAN: That's right, they mostly made milk. And apples too, and pears. Sheridan had the maple syrup. But it was mostly pasture and milk.

REPORTER: And did you ever farm?

RYAN: I worked for farmers, but never run a place of my own, no.

REPORTER: How come? I'm told your family once owned thousands of acres.

RYAN: That's right, six thousand more or less. I had five sisters, you see.

REPORTER: I don't understand.

RYAN: Well everytime they wanted a new hat they'd sell a couple hundred acres. We ended up with a while heap of hats but all I've got left is this three acres I'm sittin' on. Who'd you rather work for, Jew or Italian?

REPORTER: ...I have no idea, who would you?

RYAN: Jew. Jew'll pay you.

REPORTER: I'm Jewish.

RYAN: Oh? Well, no offense, you couldn't help it.

REPORTER: I guess you're of Irish decent.

RYAN: I guess so—my name's Ryan.

REPORTER: I believe your people first came here around the Irish potato famine of 1848?

RYAN: No, before that,—the regular famine.

REPORTER: I understand you worked right into your nineties. What were you doing?

RYAN: That would depend on who was watchin'. (*Laughs.*) After the farms give out I mowed lawns for the city people, rakin' leaves come Fall. Last few years I mostly worked for Doctor Campbell— first house bottom of the hill.

REPORTER: You suppose I could talk to him?

RYAN: You could try but he died three years ago. (*Leans toward her, lowered voice, with a glance right and left.*) Won't be missed.

REPORTER: Oh. He treat you badly?

RYAN: Campbell never treated anybody, he was tighter than a witch's...well, no use goin' into that.

REPORTER: I'm interested in how it was, living here fifty years ago. Could you talk about that?

RYAN: Fifty wasn't too different; seventy was, though, eighty, ninety...

REPORTER: You can remember ninety years ago?

RYAN: Sure I do, what do you want to know?

REPORTER: Well, for instance—I suppose these roads were all dirt.

RYAN: Oh yes—they only paved the State Highway in 1932, 33...that was the WPA. My brother worked on that.

REPORTER: And how did you get to town when it snowed—there were no plows then, were there?

RYAN: Never bothered with the road once it snowed; you went right across country with the horses. It was quicker. Had to bring the milk to town every three days, y'see.

REPORTER: But in really deep snow?

RYAN: You'd start up here and shovel out in front of the horses till you got to the woods. Snow never gets real deep in the woods.

REPORTER: How far'd you have to shovel?

RYAN: Depends—half a mile, mile.

REPORTER: God! Takes about ten minutes to town now, how long'd it take you then?

RYAN: In Winter?—about three, three-and-a-half hours. But comin' back up was faster, bein' you had your path all cut.

REPORTER: I bet you were hungry when you got down there.

RYAN: Well, you might carry a chunk of smoked bacon in your pocket. —Might not, though.

REPORTER: That's very interesting.—I notice you have quite a bit of junk out front there.

RYAN: Oh no, that's not junk, that's just nothing. I *used* to have *real* junk, but I got to where I couldn't lift. Anyways, the State Police give me so much trouble I had to give it up.

REPORTER: Why'd they give you trouble?

RYAN: Well, you supposed to have a license to sell junk, specially auto parts.

REPORTER: Couldn't you get one?

RYAN: Never tried; don't believe in it. Never wanted the Government to have my name. They wanted me to mow lawns for the school one time, but I'd have had to put my name down for social security. Next thing they'll be comin' around for income tax or something.

REPORTER: You're really not on any government form?

RYAN: Nope. U.S. Government don't know I exist. Not the FBI, not the CIA; here I've been around a hundred years and none of them even knows I was born.

REPORTER: Well, that's kind of wonderful.

RYAN: Dr. Campbell used to say he'd have done the same thing if he'd thought of it in time. Well...I thought of it in time.

REPORTER: Don't you believe in *any* tax?

RYAN: Well, let's see. *(Pause.)* Can't think of any.

REPORTER: Tell me, were you in any of the wars?

RYAN: Nope, missed every one of them. I was always too young or too old. But you might have heard what old man Cartwright said—he had that big farm on the North side of Route... *(Realizes.)*...Well, it's gone now, but it was way back in the woods, y'see...

REPORTER: What did he say?

RYAN: Well, the first War had just started—back in...was that 1914?

REPORTER: Yes, the First World War.

RYAN: Yes. Well, Cartwright only come down into town every couple months or so, and this time he stepped off his wagon in front of the store and met a fella and they got talking and the fella said, "Ain't it a terrible thing the way they're killing each other by the thousands over there in Europe?" And old man Cartwright says, "What are they doin' that for?" And the fella says, "Haven't you heard?—they've got a world war goin' on over there." Well, old Cartwright looks up in the sky—it was a beautiful summer's morning, and not a cloud up there, and not too hot either, and he says, "Well, they've got a nice day for it!" *(They laugh together.)* You can ask me more, I'm not due anywhere.

REPORTER: It must have been pretty isolated up here in those days...did it seem that way to you?

RYAN: Personally? I don't know—I tell you, my best friend for a long time when I was a young fella was Fred Thompson, used to live over there by Haven's Bridge? And he was a couple of years older and they took him for the first War. And when he came back I asked him, and he'd been to New York and France and all over, and he said I hadn't missed much.

REPORTER: But you must have felt some attraction for the city as a young man.

RYAN: I went to Hartford once. But there was no place to sit down.

REPORTER: But didn't you want to see shows in the city? And what about women there? Weren't you curious?

RYAN: Well I don't think I can say a thing like this front of a woman.

REPORTER: Don't be shy, go ahead.

RYAN: Well, they used to say they was all dancers, the women in New York City.

REPORTER: Dancers?

RYAN: Dance on one foot, then dance on the other and make a living between them.—Sorry, I didn't mean any offense…

REPORTER: *(Rigidly.)* Well I asked you to tell me and you did. What about newspapers…did you get to read any?

RYAN: Oh, every few days. Of course I got up to Canterbury more often in later years when I was selling my junk there, and I did see one or two of those old fashioned shows they had there.

REPORTER: What do you mean?

RYAN: Well, you know—where these actors come on the stage and talk.

REPORTER: You mean plays.

RYAN: The old-time shows. I see one or two when I bring my junk up to Canterbury.—Had a awful time avoiding the cops, though. But one day…I was in my eighties then, or just about…and I had this great big Oldsmobile rear end sticking out the back of my truck 'cause it was too long to get into the car. And I stopped at the store for a loaf of bread, and when I come out this State Cop, John Burnside, is standing behind the car looking down at this rear end…naturally he knew I didn't have no license for auto parts. And I come to get into the car, and he says, "Hya Bob," and I said, "Hya John," and he says, "Nice day," and I said—"It was." *(Laughs.)* And that was the end of my junk business.

REPORTER: I'm trying to visualize the area without so many houses up here—what'd you used to see from this porch?

RYAN: Well, Isaacson's farm was down there about a mile and nothing between here and his barns; and Jonas Bean's place was out that way but you couldn't see it through the trees…fire a rifle pretty near anywhere and no danger to anybody. I made my living hunting fox through World War II. Four dollars a skin.

REPORTER: How many could you get in a day?

RYAN: Many as three a night, maybe—hunt at night for fox; in fact, I was walkin' down that road out there one night looking for fox; and I had this bright moon, and I remember thinking how they were bombing London at the time especially when the moon was bright—and I hears this sawing.

REPORTER: Sawing?

RYAN: That's right—zim, zim, zim—and I come around the pond up there, and it's gettin' closer. Who could be sawin' wood in the middle of the night? And then I see this Polack in the moonlight, sawing off this horse's head right there in the middle of the road.

REPORTER: Good God—why!

RYAN: Well, it'd dropped dead and he had no horse or tractor to move it with, so he cut it up for his pigs.

REPORTER: And where was this?

RYAN: Opposite the pond, where that piano player lives...

REPORTER: Sokolow's house!

RYAN: Well yes, but it was no mansion like it is now...the Polack kept pigs under the porch.

REPORTER: No pigs under that porch now.

RYAN: Oh, no pigs allowed at all in the township now. No roosters either, y'know—liable to wake people up before noon. *(Chuckles in reminiscence.)* I don't know why it reminds me, but just up the road from there Bruce Tynan had his farm. And he decided to get married when he turned sixty. His father was Charley, about in his eighties then and ate nothin' but raw clams...had no teeth, y'see. Old Charley stank a lot, specially in summer carryin' those clams around in his pocket, but that's here nor there. But old Bruce got married and one weekend he had this shivaree...

REPORTER: What's a shivaree?

RYAN: Don't know a shivaree?

REPORTER: I never heard the word.

RYAN: Wedding celebration. It goes on...well, till everybody drops out. They kept going a night and a day and on the second night... Bruce was kind of proper, you know, went to church and all...makin' up for all the men he killed in the first War. And I turned around, and my arm knocked over this bottle of whiskey, and old Bruce stood there lookin' at this puddle on the floor, and he says, *(Gruffly.)* "I'd rather see a church burn than waste good whiskey." *(Laughs, shaking his head.)* Old Bruce...

REPORTER: And what about church, were you religious?

RYAN: Well, my father was in the Winter.

REPORTER: Only in the Winter?

RYAN: Well, there was too much to do in the good weather. One winter was so cold—before I was born, this was—my father didn't show up in church four or five Sundays so they sent up a committee to see if there was something wrong. And when they got there they found my grandfather laid out in the front parlor. He'd been dead for three weeks but the ground was frozen three feet down and my father couldn't dig a grave.

REPORTER: It must have been pretty cold in your house.

RYAN: Oh, you could say that.

REPORTER: Still, it sounds like a pretty good life around here.

RYAN: Well, we certainly had a lot of characters. There was somebody peculiar in darn near every house. Maybe there still is but I don't know them anymore. Like old Stanley Beach who ran the general store. This woman...Russel Pound's widow...they were well-to-do, and she always had to have her stuff delivered. This was way back before the first War, and I was a young fella and I'd work for Beach now and then when he was shorthanded. And one morning she comes in—Russel Pound's widow...and orders a spool of sewing thread. And Stanley Beach says, "Will that be all?" And she says, "Yes. Will you deliver it?" And Beach says, "Why certainly, Mrs. Pound, I'd be happy to." Well, she leaves, and he goes out to his team, those horses must've been fifteen hands high, and hitches them to his big lumber wagon that was at least twenty feet long—they used to carry logs to the sawmill on it—and then he sets the spool on the wagon bed and drives up to her house and doesn't he back that enormous wagon right up to her front door; and he knocks and she comes and opens it and he sort of raises his arm out toward the spool and says, "Where do you want it?" *(They both laugh together.)* I don't know why, but you just don't hear things like that anymore.

REPORTER: Will it ever happen again, people living like that?

RYAN: Well, if you notice when you go down to town—most of the old houses on Main Street has those big porches?

REPORTER: They're lovely, yes. They're sort of inviting.

RYAN: Well you know—once upon a time people used to sit on them. Right on Main Street. And talk back and forth from one house to another. You don't see that anymore.

REPORTER: Why is that? They want privacy more now?

RYAN: I couldn't say.

REPORTER: Tell me, Mr. Ryan, when you look out at all these houses in every direction, and the cars going up and down the road out there, and all the people around—what goes through your mind?

RYAN: Tell you the truth, I do wonder sometimes—being' there's so many of them and they're moving so fast—I wonder how do they get to meet anybody.

REPORTER: Would you mind if I took a picture of us together?

RYAN: No, not at all. Where do you want me?

REPORTER: Just stay right there. *(She draws closer and aims the lens at the two of them together. Clicks.)* Just one more. Smile. *(Clicks.)* Happy birthday Mr. Ryan.

RYAN: Thank you.

(Blackout.)

END OF PLAY

Water and Wine
by Stuart Spencer

BIOGRAPHY

Stuart Spencer is the author of numerous one-act and two-act plays, including *Blue Stars, Sudden Devotion* and *Go To Ground*, which have been produced in New York at EST, where he is a member. He has written one screenplay, *White Gold*, on commission and is currently at work on another. Mr. Spencer teaches playwriting in private classes at Sarah Lawrence College and at the EST Institute for Professional Training. He also teaches dramaturgy at the Playwright's Horizons Theatre School/NYU Program and is a member of the Dramatists Guild.

AUTHOR'S NOTE

Outside Florence there is a small village called Castelfranco that sits at the base of a very large Tuscan hill. Some would call it a mountain. You can drive to the top of the hill by car, though a little more than halfway up the road turns to dirt and rock. It is the same track, one imagines, used by horses and carts for many hundreds of years.

Coming around the last bend of this single lane path, you can see a large stone farmhouse perched on the final plateau of the hill. It is fronted by a great stone wall holding back the hillside. Once you have reached the farmhouse and stand at its front door you can turn around and see the Arno Valley spread out below you like a great Tuscan table loaded with food and flowers. Around to the side of the house is the entrance to the cellar, half buried into the side of the steeply rising hill. Inside are scattered bottles, an ancient wine press, and the miscellaneous leavings of the wine makers who were this farm's occupants for many centuries.

I write the brief description of this place so that the reader will know that it was this highly personal, one could even say sensual, experience that was the inspiration for this play. For while the essential incident with which *Water and Wine* is concerned—the identification of the *Laocoon* by Michelangelo Buonarroti and Giuliano Da Sangallo—is historically accurate, the play is a work of the imagination. There are many factual inaccuracies in the text. Some are glaring (the farm was just outside Rome, not Florence), others more subtle (the farmer was paid an annuity, not a lump sum). Some I was aware of as I was writing the play, others have been brought to my attention since.

The play, in any case, is not a "historical drama" in our modern sense of the term, meaning that it's primary attempt is not to portray history. Instead, I have (attempted anyway) to use history to my own purposes. Whatever was historically convenient was used; whatever was not was discarded or changed. I shaped and selected my raw material so that I was free to explore certain ideas about both art, and the mysterious nexus between love (romantic and familial) and the creation of that art.

And also, it now occurs to me, so that I could relive in some shadowy way the beauty and simplicity and grace of an old farmhouse at the top of a very large Tuscan hill.

ORIGINAL PRODUCTION

Water and Wine was first produced at The Ensemble Studio Theatre Marathon 1995, 18th Annual One-Act Play Marathon. It was directed by Nicholas Martin (stage manager, Gregg W. Brevoort) with the following cast:

Giovanni...Ed Setrakian
Enrico ....Justin Theroux
Giuliano ....Frank Biancamano
Buonarroti ....Chris Ceraso

CHARACTERS
GIOVANNI
ENRICO
GIULIANO
BUONARROTI

TIME
Late winter, 1506.

SETTING
A farm outside Florence.

WATER AND WINE

The dark interior of a vaulted chamber. It is used as the storage room for a vineyard, so there is a large wooden vats and an array of bottles—some of them full and corked, others empty.

There are two exits, both heavy wooden doors. The first goes to the outside. The second, upstage, leads to a "cellar" which is burrowed into the side of the hill, so you don't have to descend steps to get into it. The cellar door is locked.

It is late afternoon on a winter's day. Outside it is cold and rainy. The light is beginning to fail. A single candle is on the table. It brings a warm glow to the otherwise dank room. But we can hear the wind and the rain whipping against the side of this stone structure, buried half beneath the ground.

The year is 1506. We are on a farm outside Florence.

The door bangs open and a man enters. He is in his sixties, but the farmer's life has made him look much older. He has a beard, and is weathered and grey.

Behind him will follow Enrico, in his early twenties. He's very handsome and energetic, and very earnest.

GIOVANNI: Christ! What a day! *(He sees the door is still open.)* Close the door for God's sake!
(Enrico reaches back and closes the heavy wooden door.)
ENRICO: The rain is good for the grapes, though.
GIOVANNI: It's bad for the old men.

ENRICO: In the summer, you'll by happy we had so much rain. You'll be dancing around the wine press singing songs to the Madonna.

GIOVANNI: If I live that long.

ENRICO: You say that every year.

GIOVANNI: Every year I could die. And I have never danced around any wine presses. Light a candle.

ENRICO: It's lit. Liccia must have come down.

GIOVANNI: That's it? That's the only candle we have?

ENRICO: They're expensive, papa.

GIOVANNI: Well, we've got money now, don't we.

ENRICO: Do we?

GIOVANNI: Well, as soon they get here and take a look at it. I think they'll pay plenty, don't you?

ENRICO: I don't know. I hope so.

GIOVANNI: Ah well, there you go. Hope. You add faith and charity, and you've got yourself a Beatitude.

ENRICO: Faith, hope, and charity are not Beatitudes.

GIOVANNI: No? What are they?

ENRICO: They're just three good things to have. The greatest of them is charity.

GIOVANNI: Oh forgive me, I'm just an ignorant old man.

ENRICO: Just because I go to church and you don't...

GIOVANNI: The last time I went to church that crazy Savanarola got up in the pulpit and scared me half to death.

ENRICO: They say he's not so frightening since they burned him at the stake.

GIOVANNI: And a good thing too.

ENRICO: Savanarola had some good things to say.

GIOVANNI: Why don't you march down into town and say that to the nearest Medici who happens to be walking by? I understand they've got a few stakes left and kindling is cheap.

ENRICO: That's exactly my point. The Family would do just that.

GIOVANNI: So would Savanarola.

(Enrico dismisses him with a wave.)

ENRICO: Oh—you're an old man.

GIOVANNI: You only noticed just now? Where are the candles?

(Giovanni is looking for them in a low cabinet against a wall.)

ENRICO: One is plenty.

GIOVANNI: We're going to have money soon. You wait and see. We'll have candles, some new clothes, maybe a helper for that lovely sister of your's so she doesn't complain all the time about the work she has to do.

ENRICO: Papa…

GIOVANNI: I'm sorry.

ENRICO: We agreed.

GIOVANNI: Yes, yes. I'm sorry.

ENRICO: Liccia works very hard.

GIOVANNI: God knows she works harder than your mother ever did. Now there was a lazy one.

ENRICO: Papa, that's not nice!

GIOVANNI: It's true!

ENRICO: Yes, but you don't say that about the dead.

GIOVANNI: You say what's true about the dead and let the dead take care of themselves. Anyway, they're dead. What do they care?

ENRICO: You're a wicked old man.

GIOVANNI: Yes and you are young and stupid. So when they get here, you let me do the talking. I plan to get our money's worth out of this little artifact we've discovered. (*He has found three candles. He sits at the table, and sets about putting them in holders and lighting them.*)

ENRICO: Little artifact!

GIOVANNI: Yes, exactly.

ENRICO: Oh papa! It's sculpture!

GIOVANNI: I'm not impressed by words, I'm sorry.

ENRICO: Maybe because you don't understand it.

GIOVANNI: Oh! God save us! And you do, I suppose.

ENRICO: No, but I admit it. I'm humble in my ignorance.

GIOVANNI: It's a very pretty piece of stone, I'll give you that. But all this hub-bub about art? That's for the Medici and the Pope and all those city folks who love to stroll around town gasping at all their lovely belongings. Me, I go into the vineyard every day and do my job. And do you know what? When they sit down to their table in the afternoon, they enjoy a very fine wine because of my work. Wine that in my ignorant opinion is every bit a thing of beauty as any of their fancy art.

ENRICO: Our work.

GIOVANNI: You're right—because the one thing you do know how to do is when to pick the grape.

ENRICO: Thank you.

GIOVANNI: No small talent, that. Not just anyone can time it the way you can. We make good wine because of that.

ENRICO: Thank you Papa.

GIOVANNI: A serious, businesslike exchange of cash is all I'm looking for. No elegant talk for me, if you please.

ENRICO: You're a terrible philistine.

GIOVANNI: I don't even know what that is, so it can't possibly bother me that I am one.

ENRICO: It's in the Bible.

GIOVANNI: This explains why I don't know.

ENRICO: Anyway, we'll both going do the talking.

GIOVANNI: I don't think we're having this discussion.

ENRICO: Both of us, Papa.

GIOVANNI: You don't know the first thing about business.

ENRICO: And you don't know anything about art.

GIOVANNI: I don't need to know anything.

ENRICO: For this, it wouldn't hurt.

GIOVANNI: I'm the head of this family and I do the business.

ENRICO: You could give something away and not even know it.

GIOVANNI: We've got one item on the block: a statue. We're trying to get two thousand for it, tops. We'll settle for one. I know the difference between 1,000 and 2,000. That much business sense I know I have.

ENRICO: Papa, please. Just don't close any deals without checking with me first.

GIOVANNI: I'll see how it goes. (*He goes to the upstage door and tests it. It's locked.*)

ENRICO: Papa...

GIOVANNI: I said I'll see. Now leave it. When does he get here?

ENRICO: I don't know. And it's they.

GIOVANNI: They?

(*Enrico sits at the table.*)

ENRICO: There are two of them. Buonarroti and a friend of his.

GIOVANNI: Another artist?

ENRICO: I don't know.

GIOVANNI: Maybe a businessman.

ENRICO: Maybe.

GIOVANNI: Maybe someone from the government.

ENRICO: Maybe, I don't know.

GIOVANNI: Maybe a Medici.

ENRICO: I doubt it.

GIOVANNI: Why?

ENRICO: They don't even know what we have yet. They may not be interested.

GIOVANNI: Not interested?! Are you serious?

ENRICO: They haven't seen it yet, papa.

GIOVANNI: Yes, but you described it to them in your letter, didn't you? You made that little drawing of it.

ENRICO: I'm sure my drawing looked very simple to the likes of Buonarroti.

GIOVANNI: I thought it looked very nice.

ENRICO: You're my father.

GIOVANNI: Yes, but I don't like you enough to compliment you if you don't deserve it. That was a good drawing.

ENRICO: Thank you.

(Giovanni goes to him.)

GIOVANNI: I always thought you had talent.

ENRICO: Thank you.

GIOVANNI: Who knows? With a little instruction, maybe you could be a real artist.

ENRICO: It takes more than a little instruction, Papa. It takes a long time and hard work.

GIOVANNI: Well, you were always lazy.

ENRICO: I am not lazy!

GIOVANNI: Okay, all right.

ENRICO: You know that you need me here, Papa, and that's the end of it.

GIOVANNI: I was only saying…

ENRICO: We've been through this a hundred times.

GIOVANNI: If you'd let me get a word in…

ENRICO: Let's just drop it! *(Enrico gets up and crosses away from Giovanni, though he soon realizes he has nowhere to go and ends up floating on the other side of the room.)*

GIOVANNI: I never heard of anyone finding a piece like this, have you?

ENRICO: Well, no. But we don't get much news up on this mountain-side, papa.

GIOVANNI: They're always digging up a piece of this, a chunk of that.

But a whole statue? In virtually the same condition as the day it was finished? Now that's a rare thing indeed.

ENRICO: You may be right. I hope you are.

GIOVANNI: You and that hope again.

ENRICO: I'm only saying that I don't know.

GIOVANNI: And not just any old statue, but a great one. I mean, that is one very impressive piece of marble, don't you think? So dramatic. The way they're all tangled up in the snakes like that, struggling to get free. It's pathetic, really, if you think about it. Really, very touching.

ENRICO: You sound like you almost like it.

GIOVANNI: *(Indignantly.)* I do.

ENRICO: I thought you couldn't care less about all that fancy art nonsense.

GIOVANNI: I don't care about all the nonsense. But I like the statue. It's…I don't know. It's good. It's nothing to get excited about it, but it's good. I never said it wasn't good.

ENRICO: You said you weren't impressed by it.

GIOVANNI: I never said such a thing.

ENRICO: You did. You just said it a few minutes ago.

GIOVANNI: You don't listen. I said I wasn't impressed by all the nonsense that goes with it. Of course I'm impressed by the statue. Who wouldn't be? You'd have to be blind. Or stupid. What do you take me for anyway? A philistine?

(Enrico goes to the table with the wine bottles on it.)

ENRICO: I'm going to have a little. How about you?

GIOVANNI: Unlike my son, I try not to drink up the profits.

ENRICO: So you won't have another after this cup.

GIOVANNI: Exactly.

(Enrico hands him a cup of wine.)

GIOVANNI: You're not such a bad son.

(There's a pounding at the door.)

GIOVANNI: It's them.

ENRICO: I'll get it.

GIOVANNI: Don't forget, I do the talking. *(More pounding.)* Come in! Now be obedient for once in your life.

ENRICO: Yes, papa.

(Two men enter. The first, Buonarroti, is about thirty. He is bearded and not very attractive. He is overbearing in his manner, abrupt and

arrogant. The second man, Giuliano da Sangallo, is in his forties. He is quite straight-forward, businesslike. They are both very wet and wind-blown.)

GIULIANO: God in heaven! The wind on this mountain!

GIOVANNI: Bad day out there.

GIULIANO: Terrible!

GIOVANNI: Let me take your cloaks. Enrico, some help here.

GIULIANO: Yes, yes, thank you so much.

(Meanwhile, Enrico has stepped in to take Buonarotti's cloak. Buanarotti's eyes fasten on Enrico, who manages—barely—to meet the gaze. Buonarotti's tone is stern and formal.)

BUONARROTI: You didn't tell us it was so far up the hill.

ENRICO: It's a steep climb, yes.

BUONARROTI: Look at this. I'm soaked through.

ENRICO: I'll get you some dry clothes if you like.

BUONARROTI: No, no, don't bother. I'm not staying that long.

GIOVANNI: We thought you might stay for dinner.

BUONARROTI: We have to get back.

GIULIANO: I don't know. Dinner doesn't sound so bad to me.

BUONARROTI: I want to be back in the city tonight.

GIULIANO: We're going to have to eat somewhere.

ENRICO: Yes—please stay. It would be such an honor for us to have you...

BUONARROTI: I'm not staying for dinner!

GIOVANNI: If he doesn't want to stay he doesn't have to.

BUONARROTI: I just want to look at the statue. That's what I came for.

ENRICO: Of course, of course. I only meant that...

BUONARROTI: I know what you meant.

GIOVANNI: We let our guests do what they like.

BUONARROTI: Thank you.

GIOVANNI: You don't want to eat my daughter's delicious cooking, there's nobody here to force you. My name is DeAngelo. This is my son Enrico. He's the friendly one.

BUONARROTI: I'm Buonarroti.

(Giuliano steps forward to shake hands.)

GIULIANO: Giuliano Da Sangallo. It's a pleasure. The Family would like you to know that they are very pleased you told them first of your discovery.

ENRICO: We knew that they'd appreciate the value of a great work like this.

GIOVANNI: And have the money to pay for it.

(Giuliano is a little embarrassed by this.)

GIULIANO: Yes, yes of course.

BUONARROTI: May we see the statue?

GIOVANNI: It's right in there. *(He indicates.)* We put it in the cellar—it's got the only door we can lock.

GIULIANO: Very smart.

BUONARROTI: You didn't tell anyone else about it, did you?

GIOVANNI: We're peasants up here, you know—not idiots.

GIULIANO: Oh he didn't mean that you...

(Giovanni goes to get a candle and a key, lying on the table. He unlocks the cellar door.)

GIOVANNI: *(Interrupting.)* We didn't tell a soul. But you can never be too careful. I didn't want somebody stumbling in here and catching a glimpse of it before you arrived.—Well gentlemen? Care to have a look?

(Giuliano and Buonarroti look at each other.)

BUONARROTI: You go ahead.

GIULIANO: You're not coming?

BUONARROTI: I want to sit for a minute and clear my head. I've got too many thoughts going around in it. I won't be able to look at it properly.

GIULIANO: Well, if you insist.

BUONARROTI: I do.

GIOVANNI: All right, then. Come along. Take that candle with you.

(Giuliano takes a nearby candle. They are gone.)

ENRICO: Please, have a seat.

BUONARROTI: Thank you.

ENRICO: You're sure you don't want some dry clothes.

BUONARROTI: They'll only get wet when I go back into the rain.

ENRICO: You really can spend the night if you like.

BUONARROTI: You're very kind. No thank you.

ENRICO: Whatever you want. But I want you to know that we're not just being polite.

BUONARROTI: I understand.

ENRICO: We have a comfortable house. The beds are warm and dry and they don't have lice. My sister's cooking is really very good—everybody says so, even my father, and he isn't one to give compliments. I don't understand why you'd want to go back tonight in the rain. It'll be dark soon, too.

BUONARROTI: Maybe I like the dark.

(This stops Enrico short. He turns away vaguely until his eye falls on the wine bottles.)

ENRICO: Would you like a glass of wine?

BUONARROTI: Is it your own?

ENRICO: We grow the grapes right out on that hillside.

BUONARROTI: I'll try a cup.

(Enrico pours two cups.)

ENRICO: I think we make a good wine up here. Very light. But with a good body. *(He hands Buonarroti the cup.)* But you tell me.

(Buonarroti drinks it down.)

BUONARROTI: It's fine.

ENRICO: You barely tasted it.

BUONARROTI: I thought it was fine.

ENRICO: You couldn't possibly know, drinking it that fast.

BUONARROTI: I know everything I have to know.

ENRICO: Then you don't really care about good wine.

BUONARROTI: You're right, I don't. Now please, leave me alone for a minute.

ENRICO: To clear your mind.

BUONARROTI: Yes.

ENRICO: The way a wine drinker will clear his palate. So that you're ready to have the experience.

BUONARROTI: That's right.

ENRICO: That's the only thing that's important to you.

BUONARROTI: Yes.

ENRICO: Sometimes, I draw. Papa tells me I'm very good.

BUONARROTI: For a man who doesn't hand out many compliments, he seems to do it rather often.

ENRICO: I might have gone to Florence to study.

BUONARROTI: Why didn't you?

ENRICO: I thought I should stay on the farm. My father needed the help.

BUONARROTI: We all make choices.

ENRICO: The drawing of the statue that we sent you. Did you bring it?

BUONARROTI: Yes.

ENRICO: May I see it?

BUONARROTI: It's in the cloak. Probably soaked through.

(Enrico goes to the cloak, rummages through the pockets, and produces a rolled piece of paper. He spreads it on the table.)

ENRICO: Do you mind?

BUONARROTI: Mind?

ENRICO: Giving me a critique?

BUONARROTI: You drew this?

ENRICO: Yes.

BUONARROTI: It's not bad.

ENRICO: Do you think?

BUONARROTI: You must practice.

ENRICO: Oh yes, in my spare time. In the winter, mostly. When the weather is like this.

BUONARROTI: I meant you *ought* to practice. More.

ENRICO: Oh.

BUONARROTI: The modeling of the flesh is abrupt, here. You see? You can bring out the sense of muscle, of weight. Don't pass over it as though it isn't there. It's there. Acknowledge it.

ENRICO: I see. Anything else?

BUONARROTI: That's all.

ENRICO: That's the only criticism you have?

BUONARROTI: Yes.

ENRICO: You're very kind.

BUONARROTI: No I'm not.

ENRICO: Then you really mean it. You think I have talent.

BUONARROTI: I don't know what talent is. You can draw.

ENRICO: Enough to go to Florence? To study?

BUONARROTI: That I have no idea.

ENRICO: If you don't know, who does?

BUONARROTI: You want to make it a matter of talent. I'm only saying that I don't know if talent is so important. There's a lot that goes into being an artist besides talent. Personality. Luck. Skill…

ENRICO: But you said I had skill.

BUONARROTI: There's skill and there's technique.

ENRICO: But that's what I would learn if I studied, wouldn't I?

BUONARROTI: I suppose so.

ENRICO: Then you do think I have something.

BUONARROTI: Yes.

(There obviously is something else on his mind. Enrico senses it.)

ENRICO: *What.*

BUONARROTI: Don't go to Florence. Don't study painting.

ENRICO: Why not?

BUONARROTI: It would be selfish. Your father needs you.

ENRICO: If I were a successful artist I could support my father. He'd never have to work again.

BUONARROTI: And you might fail miserably. Most artists fail miserably. Even some of the bad ones. Better to stay at home and make wine.
(Enrico lets this sink in for a moment. It's depressing, not the answer he wanted.)

ENRICO: Did you want some more?

BUONARROTI: I've had enough, actually.

ENRICO: You don't like it?

BUONARROTI: It's all right.

ENRICO: That's what you said about my drawing.
(Buonarroti shrugs.)

ENRICO: Well, maybe you just don't like good wine.

BUONARROTI: I know good wine, believe me. This isn't good. It's heavy and bitter.

ENRICO: You don't know what you're talking about.

BUONARROTI: I know how something tastes.

ENRICO: You may be a great artist, but I am a winemaker. We have the finest wine in the region on this farm. We're small, we're not famous. But the wine is good.

BUONARROTI: Have it your way. My way, it's heavy and bitter.
(A pause.)

ENRICO: Why do you have to be so unkind?

BUONARROTI: Why do you have to be so beautiful?

ENRICO: Excuse me?

BUONARROTI: You heard me.

ENRICO: I don't know what to say…

BUONARROTI: Try answering the question.

ENRICO: I don't know what you mean…

BUONARROTI: I asked you why are you beautiful. It's a simple enough question, isn't it? You answer mine, I'll answer yours. Why. Are. You. Beautiful.

ENRICO: First of all, I don't happen to think I'm so…

BUONARROTI: Just answer the question.

ENRICO: I look the way I am because…because that's who I am. Because that's how God made me. I had nothing to do with it.

BUONARROTI: Good answer.

ENRICO: Now you. You answer mine.

BUONARROTI: Isn't it obvious? The same reason. I'm not a nice person because God made me that way. *(Buonarroti takes a drink of wine.)* Oh come now, don't look so glum. Your wine is not to my taste. What could be simpler.

(Enrico gets up and puts the wine back on the low cabinet.)

ENRICO: Don't bother taking back your words.

BUONARROTI: I'm not taking them back. I'm explaining them. I told you the truth and you didn't want to hear it. That's my business, after all—telling the truth. You probably never thought of it, but what I do isn't about chipping away at blocks of marble and dabbing paint onto plaster. It's about telling the truth. Everything else is just technique. I've gotten very good at it, as you may have heard. And once you get good at something it's hard to break the habit. And if the truth is unkind, well, then so be it. Or Amen, as they say in church.

ENRICO: Do you go to church?

BUONARROTI: My dear, I *build* churches.

ENRICO: You're a liar.

BUONARROTI: No, I really do. I've already built a chapel for the San Lorenzo. I'm going to build a church for the Pope in Rome if they ever get the old one torn down. In the meantime I'm going to paint the ceiling of the Pope's chapel, which I admit isn't the same as actually constructing the building itself, but believe me—after I get done with the ceiling of that chapel nobody's going to think of that building as a building. They're going to think of it as a ceiling and nothing more.

(Enrico has finally gotten furious listening to this.)

ENRICO: Are you done congratulating yourself? Because what I meant was: you're a liar about being unkind. God didn't make you that way. You're unkind because you want to be. To me, in particular. I could see it the moment you walked in.

BUONARROTI: You saw that.

ENRICO: Yes.

BUONARROTI: How observant you must be to see all that with one look.

ENRICO: Yes, because I can see things! I have an eye—just like an artist.

BUONARROTI: Oh, this again.

ENRICO: What is it, jealousy? Are you afraid that I might really be good? Is that it?

BUONARROTI: Now you flatter yourself.

ENRICO: But when you first looked at this—the first thing you said was that I could draw! That it was good!

BUONARROTI: I said it wasn't bad.

ENRICO: That I must practice. But everyone must practice! Everyone has something to learn! Even you weren't born the way you are! And for someone who grew up on a farm, this isn't bad. Where would you be now if you had grown up on this mountain? The truth is that I could learn. Anyone could learn what they need to be an artist—if they want to badly enough.

BUONARROTI: If that were true, then my donkey could write poetry and the pope would paint his own ceiling.

ENRICO: I am an artist! I know I am!

BUONARROTI: If you're so sure, then why do you keep asking me?

ENRICO: Because you are Buonarroti!

BUONARROTI: And what is that? What is Buonarroti? It's nothing! I am nothing! You are nothing also! We are both nothing! The work is the only thing that is something! More than that I cannot tell you! *(Pause.)*

ENRICO: I think you're the cruelest man I ever met.

BUONARROTI: And *I* think that sometimes, underneath cruelty, there is something very beautiful. And sometimes, in beautiful things, there can be that which is painfully cruel. *(Pause.)* And now if I might have just a glass of water. I understand the water up here in the hills is quite good.

(A noise from within. The others are returning from the cellar.)

ENRICO: *(Suddenly, without warning.)* Take me with you.

BUONARROTI: What?

ENRICO: I want to go to Florence. I don't care if I don't have talent. I want to study art. I want to study with you.

BUONARROTI: Pour me the water.

(Enrico hesitates.)

BUONARROTI: Pour.

(Enrico pours him a glass from a pitcher.)
(Giovanni and Giuliano enter from the cellar, laughing and talking. Giovanni goes to the table and blows out the candle as he talks.)

GIOVANNI: *(Exuberantly.)* No, no—it was completely by accident. Enrico was digging the new well just as I had told him, which was pretty extraordinary in itself now that I think of it, when all of a sudden he's all stooped over, digging away at something in the dirt. The minute I get there I can see from the quality of the marble itself here was something special.

BUONARROTI: *(To Giuliano.)* And is it? Special?

GIULIANO: It's special. Oh yes. It's very special. Just as Pliny describes it.

BUONARROTI: And the...condition?

GIULIANO: Intact. Completely intact.

(Overcome, Buonarroti puts his face into his hands. Enrico makes a move toward him.)

ENRICO: Are you all right?

BUONARROTI: I'm fine. Don't touch me. I'm all right.

GIOVANNI: *(To Enrico.)* Get the man some wine.

BUONARROTI: I don't want any wine.

GIOVANNI: It's very good wine. We make it our...

BUONARROTI: I don't want the wine!

GIOVANNI: I thought I'd ask.

(Buonarroti gets up.)

BUONARROTI: I want to see it now. I'm ready.

GIOVANNI: Enrico, you go with him.

BUONARROTI: No, I'll go alone.

GIOVANNI: Enrico...*(He gestures for Enrico to follow.)*

ENRICO: Here, I'll show you the way.

BUONARROTI: I'd prefer to go alone.

(Enrico takes him by the arm.)

ENRICO: It's very dark in the cellar. You can hit your head...

BUONARROTI: Get your hand off me!

GIOVANNI: Mr. Buonarroti, the statue is still mine and I want you accompanied. I'm not requesting. Understand?

(Buonarroti looks at Enrico, then back at Giovanni. Then to Enrico...)

BUONARROTI: After you.

(Enrico lights the candle, goes to the cellar door and goes inside, followed by Buonarroti.)

GIOVANNI: Some wine?

GIULIANO: I believe I will, thank you.

(Giovanni goes to the low cabinet, brings back the wine and two cups. He will pour them out. He talks through all this.)

GIOVANNI: Quite a charmer, that Buonarroti.

GIULIANO: You must forgive him. He's very decent, really, but very... unhappy.

GIOVANNI: Yes, must be tough. All those dinners with the Pope.

GIULIANO: He doesn't care about that sort of thing.

GIOVANNI: Then we're alike. Neither do I.

GIULIANO: *(Confidentially.)* He enjoys men.

GIOVANNI: Yes...?

GIULIANO: You understand what I mean? Instead of women.

GIOVANNI: You think I never heard of such a thing? I live on a farm, not the moon. *(He assumes a mock-confidential tone.)* We even have men like that around here.

GIULIANO: Well, it's against church teaching.

GIOVANNI: Hm! The church is against church teaching.

GIULIANO: I'd watch what I say! People get burned for less than that.

GIOVANNI: Oh really, who do you think you're fooling? You didn't get where you are with the Medici by being a humble servant of God.

GIULIANO: I am as humble a servant of God as the next man!

GIOVANNI: Tell it to Savanarola.

GIULIANO: I told him—he didn't listen! *(They laugh.)* You know what I wonder? I wonder what you'll do with the money.

GIOVANNI: We haven't discussed money yet.

GIULIANO: No, but we will. If I read you correctly, you want plenty.

GIOVANNI: Something wrong with that? I'll bet the Family asks for plenty when it's making its deals.

GIULIANO: Oh, they do.

GIOVANNI: Well, then.

GIULIANO: I only wonder what you'll do with it, that's all.

GIOVANNI: That depends on how much it is.

GIULIANO: Let's say you get everything you want.

GIOVANNI: I'd go down into the village and hire a couple of men and get them to come up here and tend my vines for me. Then I'd sit in my house and enjoy what's left of my life. That's not so unreasonable, is it?

GIULIANO: Not if you ask me.

GIOVANNI: My son would think so.

GIULIANO: The sculpture doesn't belong to your son.

GIOVANNI: No, but he wants me to let him bargain with you. I don't think that's such a good idea, do you?

GIULIANO: I wouldn't know.

GIOVANNI: He's young and sentimental. He doesn't know about business.

GIULIANO: Well, in that case, if you ask me, you should let him join in the bargaining as much as he wants. *(They laugh.)* I love to bargain with sentimental people!

GIOVANNI: I'll bet you do. He wants to go with you.

GIULIANO: With me?

GIOVANNI: With this Buonarroti fellow, to Florence. He wants to study art.

GIULIANO: Why didn't he just say so?

GIOVANNI: He doesn't want me to know. He's guilty about leaving the old man on the mountaintop. He thinks he's fooling me. He lies about it. "No, papa. I don't want to be an artist. I don't want to be a painter." But I know. I can see it. The more he denies it, the more I know.

GIULIANO: And you won't let him go?

GIOVANNI: I need him here on the farm, don't I.

GIULIANO: Not if you have the money from the statue.

GIOVANNI: He's not very good, though. That's the real problem. He should stay for his own sake.

GIULIANO: Yes, but if the boy wants to go...

GIOVANNI: You saw his drawing of the statue.

GIULIANO: It wasn't so bad. The boy hasn't had any training. He could be very competent if he put his mind to it.

GIOVANNI: I don't believe he's interested in "competent".

GIULIANO: Well, not everyone can be like Mr. Buonarroti here.

GIOVANNI: Tell that to Enrico. He thinks he can be.

GIULIANO: Still, he could have a career of some kind. People do. Thousands of them.

GIOVANNI: He's a dreamer. He imagines things for himself and he thinks they'll come true, but they won't. I couldn't stand him to be so disappointed.

GIULIANO: You know, honestly—and not that this makes much difference to me, one way or the other—but really, I suspect you're a selfish, lonely old man who is afraid he'll be left alone to die up here in the hills.

GIOVANNI: Maybe I am selfish. Then again, maybe selfish is a good thing, if it saves somebody else a lot of heartache and disappointment.

GIULIANO: But you can't keep him here where he doesn't want to be.

GIOVANNI: But it's not me keeping him, don't you see? It's God. Enrico prayed and asked for the gift and God said no. God does that on occasion. Have you noticed? It's God who's keeping him here, or Fate if you prefer. Like the snakes on those men in the statue. It's Fate that's dragging him down and there's nothing to do about it. *(A slight pause.)*

GIULIANO: I have a confession.

GIOVANNI: What's that?

GIULIANO: This wine has given me quite an appetite.

(Giovanni laughs.)

GIOVANNI: Come upstairs, then. We'll have dinner while we wait.

(Giovanni goes to the outside door. Giuliano starts to follow.)

GIULIANO: They won't wonder where we went?

GIOVANNI: Where is there to go? Enrico will know we're upstairs. Come on, don't worry about them. You'll like Liccia. She's very pretty, and not married yet. Tell me, Mr. Da Sangallo, are you married yourself? Because Liccia is very hard working. All day scrubbing and cooking and *(They are gone.)*

(The door to the cellar slams open. Buonarroti stands for a moment, dazed and unsure where to move. Finally he walks into the room. Enrico appears at the door behind him. He blows out the candle. He talks nervously.)

ENRICO: I knew you'd feel this way about it. I did too, the moment I saw it, I knew. Papa doesn't appreciate these things, but I—I know something great when I see it. That's what I want to do. I want to be an artist like that also!

BUONARROTI: For God's sake, just shut up, would you?! *(Pause.)* You don't understand, do you. When God made the world, he *created* something. In the truest sense, the real sense of the word: to bring into being. There was nothing, now there is something. That's what God did. We forget that—there was nothing. *Nothing.* And now…the world. The stars, the sun…*(He runs his fingers along the table top and looks at his fingertips.)*…dust, air, stones. You. I. When an artist paints, or a sculptor hammers the stone—that's not creation. We're just rearranging things. It looks new, it seems as if we've created something, but no—never. It's not possible. Only

God can create things and he's long since finished. *But...* sometimes, once in a lifetime, once in a thousand years, there is a work of man that *seems* to be new. That seems to be actually created. The material seems not to have been before, and now it is. *(He gestures behind him, to the inner door.)* That...that creation in your cellar is one of these. Laocoon[1], he's the man, the father, a Trojan priest. He reaches up to escape the serpent's grasp and... *(Unconsciously, he begins to imitate the figures in the statue.)*...his head rears back just at the moment of knowledge, the moment of despair, knowing that the reach is futile. He knows in this instant that he will die in the serpent's terrible grip. And his sons will die too. That all is lost. Yet the moment is about the *struggle*, the agonizing struggle that must go on! Now, and forever. *Now, this precise moment! And forever!* If ever man came close to God, it was in that piece of stone in your cellar. In that marble, man has created something which comes breathlessly close, heartstoppingly close to anything in God's own creation. And you casually stroll out the door and say you'd like to do that too. Well, you can't! It doesn't happen that way! Nobody can! Even *I* can't!

ENRICO: I'm sorry, I...that's not what I meant. I only meant I was inspired, to do great things.

BUONARROTI: It's fake, that kind of inspiration. You don't get inspiration from art, you get it from life. Good art only intimidates you into doing a little better.

ENRICO: I'm sorry.

BUONARROTI: You might as well learn it now. You will never, never create such a thing as that!

ENRICO: All right! I hear you!

BUONARROTI: Yes, but do you understand me?

ENRICO: Yes.

BUONARROTI: And that's the end of it? No more talk of going to Florence.

ENRICO: No, not if you say so. *(Pause.)*

BUONARROTI: I do.

(Enrico nods his head for a moment, accepting this. He picks up the bottle of wine and carries it back to a side cabinet. He pours himself a cup and drinks it before returning it to the shelf.)

ENRICO: I'm sorry if I upset you.

BUONARROTI: You didn't.

ENRICO: I think I did. I apologize.

BUONARROTI: You had to know, that's all. No one around here is able to tell you. But I could and I did. The truth, remember?

ENRICO: I meant that maybe I upset you because I reminded you of your own shortcomings.

BUONARROTI: Mine?

ENRICO: Isn't that really why you're angry? Because I reminded you that even you won't ever make anything like the statue?

(Buonarroti starts to laugh.)

ENRICO: Laugh if you want. But you weren't a minute ago. I guess we all have our limitations. I have mine, but you have yours. You told me why I'll never be an artist. But you said something about yourself at the same time, and when you heard it come out—you didn't like it very much.

BUONARROTI: Wrong! Wrong on both counts! The reason you'll never be an artist? Not because I say so. Because you listened to me when I said it! Because you didn't laugh in my face and say "Ha! Buonarroti! What do you know?!" You'll defend your wine to the death, but your passion for art? I talked you out of it in two minutes.

ENRICO: But even you could not do what that sculptor has done! You said so yourself!

BUONARROTI: No…that's right: I can't. *(He leans forward with enormous conviction.)* I can do better. I'll take what he's done and I'll go farther, I'll be greater, I'll do more. That's why I'm an artist, because I believe that I can. I might be wrong, but I believe. It's all the difference.

(The outside door opens and Giovanni enters, followed by Giuliano.)

GIULIANO: Ah, you're back! Good!

GIOVANNI: We went upstairs for a little something to eat but your lazy sister forgot to make dinner.

GIULIANO: Well? Did you see?

BUONARROTI: Yes.

GIULIANO: Good, excellent. Because we've come to an arrangement, financially speaking.

(Giovanni looks to Enrico.)

GIOVANNI: I think you'll be happy with the amount, Enrico.

GIULIANO: Three thousand, plus an order for a shipment of wine from this fine estate. *(He looks at Buonarroti.)* You don't think it's too much, do you?

BUONARROTI: The sculpture is beyond price.

GIULIANO: Just what I thought. Mr. DeAngelo drives a hard bargain but I believe everyone is pleased now.

BUONARROTI: We're lucky he doesn't want to keep it for himself.

GIULIANO: Yes, indeed. Well. Shall we go then?

BUONARROTI: Everything is done?

GIULIANO: We've signed an agreement. I'll be back up tomorrow with some workmen and a carriage. *(Pointedly, to Giovanni.)* And the money. Nothing to do tonight, but go home and get some sleep.

GIOVANNI: It's not raining so hard. And the wind is stopped.

GIULIANO: Yes, well, there you have it then.

(Buonarroti stands.)

BUONARROTI: Thank you for your hospitality. I apologize if I was abrupt, earlier. I was nervous about seeing it.

GIOVANNI: Well it's all worked out, hasn't it. Everybody's happy.

BUONARROTI: Yes, indeed. *(He goes back to Enrico.)* Do you ever come to Rome?

ENRICO: Rome?! No. Why?

BUONARROTI: I thought you might come see my chapel ceiling when it's finished. I already have ideas for it. It will be very beautiful. Not as beautiful as you, but after all, you are the original, made by God. *(He goes to the outside door.)* Come. *(He exits.)*

GIULIANO: Yes, well, good to meet. See you tomorrow, just after noon, I imagine. *(He hurries after Buonarroti. Giovanni closes the door after him. A slight beat.)*

GIOVANNI: Did he try something with you?

ENRICO: Oh Papa, for God's sake...

GIOVANNI: Listen, you bring your goods to market, sometimes you have to throw in a little something extra to close the deal.

ENRICO: He liked the statue enough all on its own.

GIOVANNI: I closed the deal without you.

ENRICO: It's all right. It doesn't matter.

GIOVANNI: Well I apologize. I said I'd wait for you.

ENRICO: You said nothing of the kind. You told me to mind my own business.

GIOVANNI: Enrico, how can you get things wrong so much? I wonder about you. I promised I'd consult you before I closed the deal. And I didn't—but for three thousand! How could I hesitate? And a shipment of wine, to be drunk by the Medici themselves!

ENRICO: I thought you couldn't care less about the Medici.

GIOVANNI: They drink a lot of wine. I could learn to care about them.
    (Enrico moves toward the door.)

ENRICO: Well you have your money, that's the important thing.

GIOVANNI: It'll be yours soon.

ENRICO: Not so soon, I don't think.

GIOVANNI: I could die anytime.

ENRICO: You've said that for years.

GIOVANNI: It's been true for years.

ENRICO: I'm going up to bed, Papa. *(He again goes to the door.)*

GIOVANNI: I got a thousand more than either of us dreamed of. Don't you want to know what I plan on doing with it?

ENRICO: What, Papa?

GIOVANNI: It's enough to send you to Florence. You could study.
    (Enrico doesn't know how to answer.)

GIOVANNI: I know it's what you want. *(Pause.)*

ENRICO: I don't think so.

GIOVANNI: What do you mean? Why not?

ENRICO: A few years ago, maybe. Not anymore.

GIOVANNI: What are you talking about? You're twenty-one years old. People learn to draw when they're twenty-one. Besides, you already know how. You only need to get better.

ENRICO: When I was younger, I think maybe then I might have become an artist. But you change, Papa. A person changes. Then it's not possible anymore.

GIOVANNI: Oh what a bunch of crap!

ENRICO: When the grape is ready to be picked, you pick it. If you wait, the grape is no good for wine. Good for other things, maybe. Not for wine. Not for a great wine. There's nothing you can do to change it. You know that, Papa.

GIOVANNI: You're not a grape.

ENRICO: I'm not an artist.

GIOVANNI: *(Shrugs.)* Well, have it your way.

ENRICO: Thank you, Papa. *(He starts to go, then stops again.)* I do know when to pick the grape, though, don't I.

GIOVANNI: Like no one I ever saw. You have the knack.

ENRICO: It's an honorable profession, winemaking.

GIOVANNI: I always thought so.

ENRICO: I know you did. Good night Papa.

GIOVANNI: Good night.

(Enrico goes out and closes the door. Giovanni goes to cabinet, gets the bottle of wine and a cup, and sits at the table. He pours a little in the cup and drinks. He likes what he tastes. He fills the cup and takes another good drink. He sighs happily. The lights fade to black.)

END OF PLAY

[1]Lay - ok′ - oh - on′.

The Wreck on the Five-Twenty-Five
by Thornton Wilder

INTRODUCTORY AND BIOGRAPHICAL NOTE

Thornton Wilder (1897–1975) had a lifelong fascination with the one-act play as a dramatic form and great success with his own shorter works. Even today, almost a century after his birth, such Wilder plays as *The Long Christmas Dinner* and *The Happy Journey from Camden to Trenton* remain staples of the one-act repertoire.

Wilder often conceived of his one-acts as discrete pieces of a larger scheme. As an undergraduate, for example, he wrote a series of *Three–Minute Plays for Three Persons*. In 1956 he began working on several one-acts that became part of a projected cycle of fourteen plays depicting the Seven Deadly Sins and the Seven Ages of Man. Sadly Wilder completed only six plays in this ambitious project—two "ages" and four "sins"—of which *The Wreck on the Five-Twenty-Five*, portraying the sin of Sloth, is an example.

With Lillian Gish and Hiram Sherman in leading roles, the play received its world premier in 1957 in West Berlin as part of the celebration surrounding the dedication of that city's new Congress Hall. Although the play received favorable notices, Wilder never again permitted it to be produced or even to be published.

In October 1994, nearly four decades after the first draft had been completed, *The Wreck of the Five-Twenty-Five* finally appeared in print in *The Yale Review* (Volume 82, Number 4). Readers interested in the history of this work as well as details about the fate of the other "sins" and "ages," are referred to the Introductory Note by Donald Gallup, Thornton Wilder's Literary Executor, in that publication.

Thornton Wilder, recognized as one of this country's most distinguished men of letters, was born in Madison, Wisconsin in 1897. After growing up in China and California, he attended Oberlin and Yale for his baccalaureate studies. After college, he spent a year studying archaeology in Rome. From that experience came his first novel, *The Cabala* (1926). He later taught French at Lawrenceville School in New Jersey, and English at the University of Chicago. In 1927 he wrote *The Bridge of San Luis Rey*, a novel which won the Pulitzer Prize and turned him overnight into a leading writer. His other novels included *The Woman of Andros, Heaven's My Destination, Ides of March* and *The Eighth Day*. His last novel, *Theophilus North*, was published in 1973.

Today, Thornton Wilder is perhaps better known from his plays, among them the Pulitzer Prize winning *Our Town* (1938) and *The Skin of Our Teeth* (1943). Wilder's *The Matchmaker* (1954), a great success with the actress Ruth Gordon, served as the basis of the hit musical *Hello Dolly!* starring Carol Channing. He also collaborated on two operas, one composed by Paul Hindemith. Collections of his essays and journals have been published since Wilder's death in Hamden, Connecticut in 1975. Currently, research is being conducted on such topics as his long friendship with Gertrude Stein and his consuming interest in the work of James Joyce.

ORIGINAL AMERICAN PRODUCTION

The Wreck on the Five-Twenty-Five was first produced at the Ensemble Studio Theatre Marathon 1995, 18th Annual One-Act Play Marathon. It was directed by Richard Lichte (stage manager, Shelli Aderman) with the following cast:

Mrs. Hawkins . . . . Deborah Hedwall
Minnie . . . . Melinda Page Hamilton
Mr. Forbes . . . . Rodney Clark
Herbert Hawkins . . . . James Murtaugh

CHARACTERS
MRS. HAWKINS
MINNIE
MR. FORBES
HERBERT HAWKINS

THE WRECK ON THE FIVE-TWENTY-FIVE

Today. Six o'clock in the evening. Mrs. Hawkins, 40, and her daughter Minnie, almost 16, are sewing and knitting. At the back is a door into the hall and beside it a table on which is a telephone.

MRS. HAWKINS: Irish stew doesn't seem right for Sunday dinner, some-how. *(Pause.)* And your father doesn't really like roast or veal. *(Pause.)* Thank Heaven, he's not crazy about steak. *(Another pause while she takes some pins from her mouth.)* I must say it's downright strange—his not being here. He hasn't telephoned for years, like that—that he'd take a later train.

MINNIE: Did he say what was keeping him?

MRS. HAWKINS: No...something at the office, I suppose. *(She changes pins again.)* He never really did like chicken, either.

MINNIE: He ate pork last week without saying anything. You might try pork chops, mama; I don't really mind them.

MRS. HAWKINS: He doesn't ever say anything. He eats what's there.— Oh, Minnie men never realize that there's only a limited number of things to eat.

MINNIE: What did he say on the telephone exactly?

MRS. HAWKINS: "I'll try to catch the six-thirty."
(Both look at their wristwatches.)

MINNIE: But, mama, papa's not cranky about what he eats. He's always saying what a good cook you are.

MRS. HAWKINS: Men! *(She has put down her sewing and is gazing before her.)* They think they want a lot of change—variety and change, variety and change. But they don't really. Deep down, they don't.

MINNIE: Don't *what?*

MRS. HAWKINS: You know for a while he read all those Wild Western magazines: cowboys and horses and silly Indians...two or three a week. Then, suddenly, he stopped all that. It's as though he thought he were in a kind of jail or prison.—Keep an eye on that window, Minnie. He may be coming down the street any minute. *(Minnie rises and turning peers through a window, back right.)*

MINNIE: No.—There's Mr. Wilkerson, though. He came back on the five-twenty-five, anyway. Sometimes papa stops at the tobacco shop and comes down Spruce Street. *(She moves to the left and looks through another window.)*

MRS. HAWKINS: Do you feel as though you were in a jail, Minnie?

MINNIE: *What?!*

MRS. HAWKINS: As though life were a jail?

MINNIE: *(Returning to her chair.)* No, of course, not.—Mama, you're talking awfully funny tonight.

MRS. HAWKINS: I'm not myself. *(Laughs lightly.)* I guess I'm not myself because of your father's phone call—his taking a later train, like that, for the first time in so many years.

MINNIE: *(With a little giggle.)* I don't know what the five-twenty-five will have done without him.

MRS. HAWKINS: *(Not sharply.)* And all those hoodlums he plays cards with every afternoon.

MINNIE: And all the jokes they make.
(Mrs. Hawkins has been looking straight before her—through a window—over the audience's heads; intently.)

MRS. HAWKINS: There's Mrs. Cochran cooking her dinner.
(They both gaze absorbedly at Mrs. Cochran a moment.)

MRS. HAWKINS: Well, I'm not going to start dinner until your father puts foot in this house.

MINNIE: *(Still gazing through the window; slowly.)* There's Mr. Cochran at the door...They're arguing about something.

MRS. HAWKINS: Well, that shows that he got in on the five-twenty-five, all right.

MINNIE: Don't people look foolish when you see them, like that—and you can't hear what they're saying? Like ants or something.

Somehow, you feel it's not right to look at them when they don't know it.

(They return to their work.)

MRS. HAWKINS: Yes, those men on the train will have missed those awful jokes your father makes. *(Minnie giggles.)* I declare, Minnie, every year your father makes worse jokes. It's growing on him.

MINNIE: I don't think they're awful, but—I don't understand *all* of them. Do you? Like what he said to the minister Sunday. I was so embarrassed I didn't want to tell you.

MRS. HAWKINS: I don't want to hear it—not tonight. *(Her gaze returns to the window.)* I can't understand why Mrs. Cochran is acting so strangely. And Mr. Cochran has been coming in and out of the kitchen.

MINNIE: And they seem to keep looking at us all the time.

(After a moment's gazing, they return to their work.)

MRS. HAWKINS: Well, you might as well tell me what your father said to the minister.

MINNIE: I...I don't want to tell you, if it makes you nervous.

MRS. HAWKINS: I've lived with his jokes for twenty years. I guess I can stand one more.

MINNIE: Mr. Brown had preached a sermon about the atom bomb...and about how terrible it would be...and at the church door papa said to him: "Fine sermon, Joe. I enjoyed it. But have you ever thought of this, Joe,"—he said—"Suppose the atom bomb didn't fall, what would we do then? Have you ever thought of that?—Mr. Brown looked terribly put out.

MRS. HAWKINS: *(Puts down her sewing.)* He said that!! I declare, he's getting worse. I don't know where he gets such ideas. People will be beginning to think he's *bitter*. Your father isn't bitter. I know he's not bitter.

MINNIE: No, mama. People like it. People stop me on the street and tell me what a wonderful sense of humor he has. Like...like... *(She gives up the attempt and says merely:)* Oh, nothing.

MRS. HAWKINS: Go on. Say what you were going to say.

MINNIE: What did he mean by saying: "There we sit for twenty years playing cards on the five-twenty-five, hoping that something big and terrible and wonderful will happen—like a wreck, for instance?"

MRS. HAWKINS: *(More distress than indignation.)* I say to you seriously,

Minnie, it's just *self-indulgence.* We do everything we know how to make him happy. He loves his home, you know he does. He likes his work—he's proud of what he does at the office. *(She rises and looks down the street through the window at the back; moved.)* Oh, it's not *us* he's impatient at: it's the whole world. He simply wishes the whole world were different—that's the trouble with him.

MINNIE: Why, mama, papa doesn't complain about anything.

MRS. HAWKINS: Well, I wish he would complain once and a while. *(She returns to her chair.)* For Sunday I'll see if I can't get an extra bit of veal. *(They sit in silence a moment. The telephone rings.)* Answer that, will you dear? —No, I'll answer it.

(Minnie returns to her work. Mrs. Hawkins has a special voice for answering the telephone, slow and measured.)

MRS. HAWKINS: This is Mrs. Hawkins speaking. Oh, yes, Mr. Cochran. What's that? I don't hear you. *(A shade of anxiety:)* Are you *sure?* You must be mistaken.

MINNIE: Mama, what is it?

(Mrs. Hawkins listens in silence.)

MINNIE: Mama!—Mama!!—What's he saying? Is it about papa?

MRS. HAWKINS: Will you hold the line one minute, Mr. Cochran? I wish to speak to my daughter. *(She puts her hand over the mouthpiece.)* No, Minnie. It's not about your father at all.

MINNIE: *(Rising.)* Then what *is* it?

MRS. HAWKINS: *(In a low, distinct and firm voice.)* Now you do what I tell you. Sit down and go on knitting. Don't look up at me and don't show any surprise.

MINNIE: *(A groan of protest.)* Mama!

MRS. HAWKINS: There's nothing to be alarmed about—but I want you to *obey* me. *(She speaks into the telephone.)* Yes, Mr. Cochran... No...Mr. Hawkins telephoned that he was taking a later train tonight. I'm expecting him on the six-thirty.—You do what you think best.—I'm not sure that's necessary but...you do what you think best.—We'll be right here. *(She hangs up and stands thinking a moment.)*

MINNIE: Mama, I'm almost sixteen. *Tell* me what it's about.

MRS. HAWKINS: *(Returns to her chair; bending over her work she speaks as guardedly as possible.)* Minnie, there's probably nothing to be alarmed about. Don't show any surprise at what I'm about to say to you. Mr. Cochran says that there's been somebody out on the lawn watching us—for ten minutes or more. A man. He's been standing in the shadow of the garage, just looking at us.

MINNIE: *(Lowered head.)* Is *that* all!

MRS. HAWKINS: Well, Mr. Cochran doesn't like it. He's...he says he's going to telephone the police.

MINNIE: The police!!

MRS. HAWKINS: Your father'll be home any minute, anyway. *(Slight pause.)* I guess it's just some...some *moody* person on an evening walk. Maybe, Mr. Cochran's done right to call the police, though. He says that we shouldn't pull the curtains or anything like that—but just act as though nothing had happened.—Now, I don't want you to get frightened.

MINNIE: I'm not, mama. I'm just...interested. Most nights *nothing* happens.

MRS. HAWKINS: *(Sharply.)* I should hope not!
(Slight pause.)

MINNIE: Mama, all evening I *did* have the feeling that I was being watched...and *that* man was being watched by Mrs. Cochran; and *(Slight giggle.)* Mrs. Cochran was being watched by us.

MRS. HAWKINS: We'll know what it's all about in a few minutes.
(Silence.)

MINNIE: But, mama, what would the man be looking at?—just us two sewing.

MRS. HAWKINS: I think you'd better go in the kitchen. Go slowly—and don't look out the window.

MINNIE: *(Without raising her head.)* No! I'm going to stay right here. But I'd like to know *why* a man would do that—would just stand and look. Is he...a crazy man?

MRS. HAWKINS: No. I don't think so.

MINNIE: Well, say *something* about him.

MRS. HAWKINS: Minnie, the world is full of people who think that everybody's happy except themselves. They think their lives should be more exciting.

MINNIE: Does that man think that out lives are exciting, mama?

MRS. HAWKINS: Our lives are just as exciting as they ought to be, Minnie.

MINNIE: *(With a little giggle.)* Well, they are tonight.

MRS. HAWKINS: They are all the time; and don't you forget it. *(The front door bell rings.)* Now, who can that be at the front door? I'll go

Minnie. *(Weighing the dangers.)* No, *you* go. —No, I'll go. *(She goes into the hall. The jovial voice of Mr. Forbes is heard.)*

MR. FORBES'S VOICE: Good evening, Mrs. Hawkins. Is Herb home?

MRS. HAWKINS'S VOICE: No, he hasn't come home yet, Mr. Forbes. He telephoned that he'd take a later train.

(Enter Mr. Forbes, followed by Mrs. Hawkins.)

MR. FORBES: Yes, I know. The old five-twenty-five wasn't the same without him. Darn near went off the rails. *(To Minnie.)* Good evening, young lady.

MINNIE: *(Head bent; tiny voice.)* Good evening, Mr. Forbes.

MR. FORBES: Well, I thought I'd drop in and see Herb for a minute. About how maybe he'd be wanting a new car—now that he's come into all that money.

MRS. HAWKINS: Come into *what* money, Mr. Forbes?

MR. FORBES: Why, sure, he telephoned you about it?

MRS. HAWKINS: He didn't say anything about any money.

MR. FORBES: *(Laughing loudly.)* Well, maybe I've gone and put my foot in it again. So he didn't tell you anything about it yet? Haw-haw-haw. *(Confidentially.)* If he's got to pay taxes on it we figured out that—even with taxes—he'd get about eighteen thousand dollars. —Well, you tell him I called, and tell him that I'll give him nine hundred dollars on that Chevrolet of his—maybe a little more after I've had a look at it.

MRS. HAWKINS: I'll tell him.—Mr. Forbes, I'm sorry I can't ask you to sit down, but my daughter's had a cold for days now and I wouldn't want you to take it home to your girls.

MR. FORBES: I'm sorry to hear that.—Well, as you say, I'd better not carry it with me. *(He goes to the door, then turns and says confidentially:)* Do you know what Herb said when he heard that he'd got that money? Haw-haw-haw. I've always said Herb Hawkins has more sense of humor than anybody I know. Why, he said—"All window-glass is the same." Haw-haw—"All window-glass is the same." Herb! You can't beat him.

MRS. HAWKINS: "All window glass is the same." What did he mean by that?

MR. FORBES: You know: that thing he's always saying. About life. He said it at Rotary in his speech. You know how crazy people look when you see them through a window—arguing and carrying on—and you can't hear a word they say? He says that's the way things look to him. Wars and politics…and everything in life. *(Mrs. Hawkins is silent and unamused.)*

MR. FORBES: Well, I'd better be going. Tell Herb there's real good glass—*unbreakable*—on the car I'm going to sell him. Good night, miss; good night, Mrs. Hawkins.
(He goes out. Mrs. Hawkins does not accompany him to the front door. She stands a moment looking before her. Then she says, from deep thought:)

MRS. HAWKINS: That's your father who's been standing out by the garage.

MINNIE: Why would he do that?

MRS. HAWKINS: Looking in.—I should have known it.

MINNIE: *(Amazed but not alarmed.)* Look! All over the lawn!

MRS. HAWKINS: The police have come. Those are their flashlights.

MINNIE: All over the place! I can hear them talking…Papa's angry…Papa's *very* angry. *(They listen.)* Now they're driving away.

MRS. HAWKINS: I should have known it. *(She returns to her seat. Sound of the front door opening and closing noisily.)* That's your father.— Don't mention anything unless he mentions it first.
(They bend over their work. From the hall sounds of Hawkins singing the first phrase of "Valencia." Enter Hawkins, a commuter. His manner is of loud forced geniality.)

HAWKINS: Well—HOW are the ladies? *(He kisses each lightly on the cheek.)*

MRS. HAWKINS: I didn't start getting dinner until I knew when you'd get here.

HAWKINS: *(Largely.)* Well, *don't* start it. I'm taking you two ladies out to dinner.—There's no hurry, though. We'll go to Michaelson's after the crowd's thinned out. *(Starting for the hall on his way to the kitchen.)* Want a drink, anybody?

MRS. HAWKINS: No.—The ice is ready for you on the shelf.
(He goes out. From the kitchen he can be heard singing "Valencia." He returns, glass in hand.)

MRS. HAWKINS: What kept you, Herbert?

HAWKINS: Nothing. Nothing. I decided to take another train. *(He walks back and forth, holding his glass at the level of his face.)* I decided to take another train. *(He leans teasingly a moment over his wife's shoulder, conspiratorially.)* I thought maybe things might look different through the windows of another train. You know: all those towns

I've never been in? Kenniston—Laidlaw—East Laidlaw—
Bennsville. Let's go to Bennsville some day. Damn it, I don't know
why people should go to Paris and Rome and Cairo when they
could go to Bennsville. Bennsville! Oh, Bennsville,—

MRS. HAWKINS: Have you been drinking, Herbert?

HAWKINS: This is the first swallow I've had since last night. "Oh,
Bennsville...breathes there a man with soul so dead—"
*(Minnie's eyes have followed her father as he walks about with smiling
appreciation.)*

MINNIE: I know a girl who lives in Bennsville.

HAWKINS: They're happy there, aren't they? No, not exactly happy, but
they live it up to the full. In Bennsville they kick the hell out of
life.

MINNIE: Her name's Eloise Brinton.

HAWKINS: Well, Bennsville and East Laidlaw don't look different
through the windows of another train. It's not by looking through
a train window that you can get at the *heart* of Bennsville. *(Pause.)*
There all we fellows sit every night on the five-twenty-five playing cards
and hoping against hope that there'll be that wonderful beautiful—

MINNIE: *(Laughing delightedly.)* Wreck!!

MRS. HAWKINS: Herbert! I won't have you talk that way!

HAWKINS: A wreck, so that we can crawl out of the smoking, burning
cars...and get into one of those houses. Do you know what you see
from the windows of the train? Those people—those cars—that
you see on the streets of Bennsville—they're just dummies.
Cardboard. They've been put up there to deceive you. What really
goes on in Bennsville—inside those houses—*that's* what's interesting. People with six arms and legs. People that can talk like
Shakespeare. Children, Minnie, that can beat Einstein. Fabulous
things.

MINNIE: Papa, *I* don't mind, but you make mama nervous when you
talk like that.

HAWKINS: Behind those walls. But it isn't only behind walls that strange
things go on. Right on that train, right in those cars.—The
damnedest things. Fred Cochran and Phil Forbes—

MRS. HAWKINS: Mr. Forbes was here to see you.

HAWKINS: Fred Cochran and Phil Forbes—we've played cards together
for twenty years. We're so expert at hiding things from one another—

we're so cram-filled with things that we can't say to one another that only a wreck could crack us open.

MINNIE: *(Indicating her mother, reproachfully.)* Papa!

MRS. HAWKINS: Herbert Hawkins, why did you stand out in the dark there, looking at us through the window?

HAWKINS: Well, I'll tell you…I got a lot of money today. But more than that I got a message. A message from beyond the grave. From the dead. There was this old lady—I used to do her income tax for her—old lady. She'd keep me on a while—God, how she wanted someone to talk to…I'd say anything that came into my head…I want another drink. *(He goes into the kitchen. Again we hear him singing "Valencia.")*

MINNIE: *(Whispering.)* Eighteen thousand dollars!

MRS. HAWKINS: We've just got to let him talk himself out.

MINNIE: But, mama, why did he go and stand out on the lawn?

MRS. HAWKINS: Sh!

(Hawkins returns.)

HAWKINS: I told her a lot of things. I told her—

MINNIE: I know! You told her that everything looked as though it were seen through glass.

HAWKINS: Yes, I did. *(Pause.)* You don't hear the words, or if you hear the words, they don't fit what you see. And one day she said to me: "Mr. Hawkins, you say that all the time: why don't you do it?" "Do what?" I said. "Really stand outside and look through some windows." *(Pause.)* I knew she meant my own…well, to tell the truth, I was afraid to. I preferred to talk about it. *(He paces back and forth.)* She died. Today some lawyer called me up and said she's left me twenty thousand dollars.

MRS. HAWKINS: Herbert!

HAWKINS: *(His eyes on the distance.)* "To Herbert Hawkins, in gratitude for many thoughtfulnesses and in appreciation of his sense of humor." From beyond the grave…It was an order. I took the four o'clock home…It took me a whole hour to get up the courage to go and stand *(he points)* —out there.

MINNIE: But, papa—you didn't *see* anything! Just us sewing!

(Hawkins stares before him—then changing his mood, says briskly:)

HAWKINS: What are we going to have for Sunday dinner?

MINNIE: I know!

HAWKINS: *(Pinching her ear.)* Buffalo steak?

MINNIE: No.

HAWKINS: I had to live for a week once on rattlesnake stew.

MINNIE: Papa, you're awful.

MRS. HAWKINS: *(Putting down her sewing; in an even voice.)* Were you planning to go away, Herbert?

HAWKINS: What?

MRS. HAWKINS: *(For the first time, looking at him.)* You were thinking of going away.

HAWKINS: *(Looks into his glass a moment.)* Far away. *(Then again putting his face over her shoulder teasingly, but in a serious voice.)* There is no "away." ...There's only "here."—Get your hats; we're going out to dinner.—I've decided to move to "here." To take up residence, as they say. I'll move in tonight. I don't bring much baggage.—Get your hats.

MRS. HAWKINS: *(Rising.)* Herbert, we don't wear hats any more. That was in your mother's time.—Minnie, run upstairs and get my blue shawl.

HAWKINS: I'll go and get one more drop out in the kitchen.

MRS. HAWKINS: Herbert, I don't like your old lady.

HAWKINS: *(Turning at the door in surprise.)* Why, what's the matter with her?

MRS. HAWKINS: I can understand that she was in need of someone to talk to.—What business had she trying to make you look at Minnie and me *through windows?* As though we were strangers. *(She crosses and puts her sewing on the telephone table.)* People who've known one another as long as you and I have are not supposed to *see* one another. The pictures we have of one another are inside.— Herbert, last year one day I went to the city to have lunch with your sister. And as I was walking along the street, who do you think I saw coming toward me? From quite a ways off?—*You!* My heart stopped beating and I *prayed*—I prayed that you wouldn't see me. And you passed by without seeing me. I didn't want you to see me in those silly clothes we wear when we go to the city—and in that silly hat—with that silly look we put on our face when we're in public places. The person that other people see.

HAWKINS: *(With lowered eyes.)* You saw *me*—with that silly look.

MRS. HAWKINS: Oh, no. I didn't look long enough for that. I was too busy hiding myself. —I don't know why Minnie's so long trying to find my shawl.

(She goes out. The telephone rings.)

HAWKINS: Yes, this is Herbert Hawkins.—Nat Fischer? Oh, hello, Nat... Oh!...All right. Sure, I see your point of view...Eleven o'clock. Yes, I'll be there. Eleven o'clock.

(He hangs up. Mrs. Hawkins returns wearing a shawl.)

MRS. HAWKINS: Was that call for me?

HAWKINS: No. It was for me all right.—I might as well tell you now what it was about. *(He stares at the floor.)*

MRS. HAWKINS: Well?

HAWKINS: A few minutes ago the police tried to arrest me for standing on my own lawn. Well, I got them over that. But they found a revolver on me—without a license. So I've got to show up at court tomorrow—eleven o'clock.

MRS. HAWKINS: *(Short pause; thoughtfully.)* Oh...a revolver.

HAWKINS: *(Looking at the floor.)* Yes...I thought that maybe it was best...that I go away...a long way.

MRS. HAWKINS: *(Looking up with the beginning of a smile.)* To Bennsville?

HAWKINS: Yes.

MRS. HAWKINS: Where life's so exciting. *(Suddenly briskly.)* Well, you get the licence for that revolver, Herbert—so that you can prevent people looking in at us through the window, when they have no business to. —Turn out the lights when you come.

END OF PLAY

Rain
by Garry Williams

BIOGRAPHY

Garry Williams lives on a farm in Indiana with his wife and two children. *Rebels*, a play he co-wrote with Steven H. Ridenour, won the 1988 Festival of Emerging Theatre and has been produced in New York, Orlando, and Indianapolis. His short play, *A Death In Bethany*, was produced in 1994 by Act One/Showtime at the Met Theatre in Los Angeles. *A Blooming of Ivy* was produced the same year by Ensemble Studio Theatre's L.A. Project at the Fountain Theatre in L.A. *Rain* has been staged at the Alliance Theatre in Burbank and The Ensemble Studio Theatre in New York.

AUTHOR'S NOTE

As I sit here in front of my computer, I find myself with very little to say about this play. It was a venture of love—and about love—and I hope that comes through in the writing.

ORIGINAL PRODUCTION

Rain was originally produced by The Alliance Repertory Company in Burbank, California, August 3, 1991. It was directed by Peter Fox (production designer, L.C. Gray III) with the following cast:

Staff	Lee Ryan
Mary	Betsy Randle
Tyler	Arnie Starkey
Lindy	Hilary Davis
Tammy	Cheri Caspari

Rain was also presented at the Ensemble Studio Theatre One-Act Play Marathon 1995. It was directed by Jamie Richards (stage manager, Bernadette McGay) with the following cast:

Tyler ....Nicholas Joy
Mary...Kristin Griffith
Staff..Richmond Hoxie
Lindy ....Carrie Luft
Tammy ....Heather Robinson

TIME
　　The present, just before dusk.

SETTING
　　A farmhouse porch.

RAIN

Lights Up. It is just before dusk. The set is bathed in the warm oranges and purples of sunset. As the play progresses, the lights dim very, very slowly. By the end of the play, we are in near total darkness.

A farmhouse porch. Paint is peeling a bit, a board here or there could be replaced, but we're not looking at a neglected old house. It's just a house due for a good painting. There are a couple of padded gliders on the porch and some old overstuffed chairs that at one time proudly occupied a living room. Now they have covers thrown over them, but look comfortable all the same.

A clothesline runs alongside the porch. Simple farm clothes hang stiffly, no breeze disturbing them. An empty basket sits waiting for them to dry.

And on the bottom step sits a boy of about fifteen. He is barefoot, wears white sweat pants and no shirt. He has his legs curled up under him and stares out into the distances of his own mind. His name is Tyler. An almost saintly smile decorates his face and an occasional laugh will bubble out of his throat. It's a sweet laugh, as if he's remembering a joke or story that was funny at no one's expense.

After a few moments of Tyler's private joy the front screen door opens and a woman walks out. She's carrying an old tin watering can. This is Mary, Tyler's mom. She's been a beautiful woman in her day, and some would say she still is. But her cheeks have become like a soft leather through her forty years of farm living, and her simple dress does little for her figure. She carries with her the strength of knowing the earth and its seasons, and of believing in things greater than she.

She stands on the porch, scanning the horizon. Tyler looks up and shares his saintly smile with her. She grins.

MARY: Hi, baby. I love you. *(She goes back to watching the horizon.)* Say a prayer for rain, would you, Tyler? *(She ruffles his hair and starts carefully watering some parched plants on the porch.)* I've never seen this. My whole life I've never seen this. It's really getting scary, Ty. You keep thinking it's got to end. It's spring, it's supposed to rain in the spring. *(She pinches a dried leaf from one, looks up.)* Do you think we did something? *(Tyler just smiles at her.)* It's supposed to rain in the spring. *(She waters the last plant, sits, and fusses with its leaves.)* It makes you wonder about some of those countries that have droughts go on forever. Thirty, forty years. Everybody starves. Flies land on their faces, trying to drink from their eyes. What did they do to deserve that? Say a prayer, would you, Tyler? *(She changes the moment by plunking on the step beside him and playfully pulling his head onto her shoulder for a second. She looks out.)* Another gorgeous sunset! Must be every shade of purple on God's palette, just spread up there in long broad brush strokes. Maybe it's the dust in the air, like they say, but it's still beautiful, don't you think?
(Then the screen door flies open. It bounces back and hits something.)
STAFF: Shit! *(The door flies open again and bounces back.)* Son of a bitch! *(Mary stands quickly and goes to the door.)* Don't even think about it. *(She stops short. The door opens again and this time the feet of a man in a wheelchair keep it from closing all the way. This is Staff, Mary's husband. He awkwardly makes his way through the door. Staff has the wiry strength of a farmer, the weather-beaten face, the iron hands. It is jarring somehow to see him in a wheelchair.)* Probably broke my goddamn toes.
MARY: Staff…*(She nods toward Tyler. Staff turns and gives him a look.)*
STAFF: Yeah, right. *(He wheels his way onto the porch.)*
MARY: Did you hurt 'em, you think?
STAFF: How would I know?
MARY: You want me to check?
STAFF: No. *(He rolls out to the railing and studies the sky.)*
MARY: They said maybe by morning.
STAFF: *(Not buying it.)* Uh-huh.

(Mary walks to one of the gliders, picks up some knitting and begins working with it. Staff stares at the sky for a few more moments. He heaves a huge sigh. Mary looks up at him but says nothing. He sighs again. She waits a moment, speaks casually.)

MARY: What did Ray want?

STAFF: You know I didn't call him.

MARY: That's twice this week he's called. I give him till Wednesday and he'll drop by.

STAFF: Whatever.

MARY: You should call him, Staff. He's probably got his feelings hurt already.

STAFF: He'll live.

MARY: We'll all live. You really should call him, though.

STAFF: Drop it, would you please?

MARY: I'm seeing Martha at the meeting tomorrow and I know she'll say something. What am I supposed to tell her?
(Staff lowers his head, struggling with a growing anger. It passes. He lifts his face to look up at the sky again.)

STAFF: They say what time tonight?

MARY: Just maybe before morning.

STAFF: They say how much?

MARY: No. Tyler and I are praying for a good one. Aren't we Ty?
(Nothing from Tyler.)

STAFF: It's gonna have to be a lot of good ones.

MARY: One of those long all-day drizzles, wouldn't that be nice? One of those cool gray days where the sky just drops down and kind of melts all day long.

STAFF: We need rain, not poetry.

MARY: Maybe we need both.

STAFF: Jesus Christ.

MARY: Staff...*(Automatically, Staff turns to look at Tyler.)*

STAFF: Excuse me, Tyler. I hope I didn't offend you.
(Mary slaps her knitting to the glider.)

MARY: Now, *that* I'm not going to tolerate from you! If you're going to start that, you can just go right back in!

STAFF: Okay. Don't get all worked up.

MARY: Well, I'm not going to tolerate it, Staff.

STAFF: I gathered that.

MARY: Well, I'm not.

STAFF: All right already! Jesus Christ!

(Mary picks up her knitting. She tries to work it, but just can't stay with it.)

MARY: So if it rains real good tonight, how bad are we hurt?

STAFF: If it rains, we'll talk about it then.

MARY: Just say it rains, how bad are we hurt?

STAFF: *(Trying to maintain.)* Mary, I don't want to say it rains if it isn't going to rain. When it rains, I'll tell you how bad we're hurt.

MARY: All right. You don't have to be hateful. I was just supposing.

STAFF: You figure if you suppose hard enough you can change something?

MARY: Probably not.

STAFF: Then why suppose?

MARY: Better than doing nothing.

STAFF: It *is* doing nothing.

MARY: I guess.

(There is a sullen silence. Then the door opens and Lindy, their seventeen-year-old daughter comes out. There is something distracted in Lindy, something distant. Even so, it's evident she brings out the best in Staff. He straightens a bit in his wheelchair.)

LINDY: Mom, can I use the car? You're not going anywhere, are you?

MARY: Hadn't planned on it. Where are you off to?

LINDY: Just out for awhile.

MARY: Just out?

STAFF: Whoa, hold on a minute, both of you. Since when do you ask your mother about using the car?

LINDY: *(Realizing.)* I'm sorry, Daddy. I just kind of got used to...you know, with you in the hospital and everything.

STAFF: Do you see me sitting here?

LINDY: Well, yeah.

STAFF: Then I must not be in the hospital, am I right?

LINDY: I'm sorry. Can I use the car?

STAFF: Depends. You going cruising for boys, no. You going to buy your old man a present, I'll think about it.

LINDY: I'll buy you a present.

STAFF: Keys are on my dresser.

MARY: *(Quietly.)* They're in my purse.

(There is a strained hush. Lindy fidgets a moment.)

LINDY: I'll get 'em. Thanks, daddy. *(She escapes the moment, darting inside.)*

STAFF: *(To himself.)* Yeah, I guess they would be.

(Mary gives this moment the reverence she thinks due, then goes on to what's really on her mind.)

MARY: I don't like her going out like this, Staff. Something's not right about it.

STAFF: Hell, she wants to be with her friends. There'd be something wrong if she didn't.

MARY: But which friends? I know for a fact she isn't seeing Tammy and Brenda and them anymore.

STAFF: Good.

MARY: Good? They've been best friends forever.

STAFF: That Tammy's a ditzy little shit. Always has been.

MARY: Don't say that, Staff.

STAFF: It's true. She's not fit to be anything but some preacher's wife someday.

MARY: You say that like it's a bad thing.

STAFF: Some little mouse that lives in a hole in the church wall. Comes out for all the functions and the good gossip.

MARY: Staff, now quit.

STAFF: Sings warbly little solos that stink and no one has the heart to tell her.

MARY: *(Giggling in spite of herself.)* That's enough of that.

STAFF: You know what I'm saying.

MARY: Still, she's a good girl. Lindy never got in trouble with her.

STAFF: A little trouble might have been good for 'em both.

MARY: Now, that isn't funny.

STAFF: I'm not trying to be funny.

(The door opens and Lindy comes out.)

LINDY: Thanks, daddy. I'll see you guys later.

STAFF: Whoa, hang on there. *(Lindy stops.)* What kind of present you gonna get your old man?

LINDY: I don't know. What do you want, a turtle sundae?

STAFF: Yeah. No, wait a minute. Get me a big slushie.

LINDY: What kind?

STAFF: I don't care. Surprise me.

LINDY: You want one, mom?

MARY: No, thanks. Get one for Tyler, though. Cherry. You want cherry, Ty? *(No response from Tyler.)* Get him a cherry, he likes cherry.

LINDY: Okay. Bye, guys. *(She starts down the steps, but freezes when Mary speaks.)*

MARY: Where are you going, honey?

LINDY: Just out.

MARY: With who?

LINDY: Mom…

MARY: What? I'm just asking. I'm not supposed to care who you're going to be with? I never heard such a thing.

STAFF: Don't worry about it. Have a good time, honey.

LINDY: Thanks, daddy. I'll see you later.

STAFF: Don't forget my slushie!

LINDY: I won't. *(She goes. We hear the sound of a car starting and driving away. There is a thick silence on the porch. Then Tyler laughs.)*

MARY: I love you, baby.

> *(The silence descends once again. Mary continues with her knitting. Staff sighs heavily. He studies the sky for awhile.)*

STAFF: Okay, let's have it. *(Nothing from Mary.)* Let's just get it over with, okay?

MARY: Why?

STAFF: Because I don't want to sit here and listen to you knit all night.

MARY: You tried to make me mad, you made me mad. Why do we have to talk about it?

STAFF: I didn't try to make you mad.

MARY: Sure you did.

STAFF: I kept you from hounding her. If that makes you mad, it'll just have to be that way.

MARY: Fine. I'm not supposed to be concerned about my daughter. How silly of me not to realize that.

STAFF: Being concerned is one thing. Making her life hell is another.

MARY: Making her life…?? Now, if that isn't the…What in the world do my fears have to do with—

STAFF: Your *fears?* What do you fear?

MARY: Now, don't go picking my words apart.

STAFF: What are your fears? What are you afraid of for Lindy tonight?

MARY: Staff, don't pick a fight, okay?

STAFF: I just want to know what you fear for our daughter.

MARY: She's a young girl, what do you think I fear?

STAFF: Youth?

MARY: Now, stop.

STAFF: Put a name to it. Call it by name and maybe it'll go away.

MARY: Don't be silly.

STAFF: Isn't that what Jesus did? Didn't he find out the name of some devil and cast it out? Name it, Mary.

MARY: I'm not going to say it out loud, if that's what you want.

STAFF: Death? Is that the big fear? You afraid she's going to die tonight?

MARY: Don't even say that.

STAFF: Just trying to help here.

MARY: Well, stop.

STAFF: How about unhappiness? You afraid of that for her?

MARY: Of course I want her to be happy. What kind of question is that?

STAFF: Loneliness? That one of them?

MARY: Let's just drop it, okay?

STAFF: I want to know what you're afraid of.

MARY: All of it! I'm her mother!

(Staff throws his head back and laughs.)

STAFF: Damn big job.

MARY: Yes it is.

(There is a lengthy silence. Staff starts in again. He is serious, but there is also an undercurrent of plain mischief.)

STAFF: Want me to tell you what you're really afraid of?

MARY: No.

STAFF: Why not?

MARY: Because it's going to be hateful. And it won't be right, either.

STAFF: Oh, it'll be right, all right.

MARY: Well, don't anyway.

STAFF: Sure you don't want to know? Might clarify some things for you.

MARY: You don't need to tell me.

STAFF: Might help, though.

MARY: No it won't.

STAFF: Sex.

(Mary closes her eyes for a moment. Then she puts her knitting on the couch and stands.)

MARY: I'm going in. Come on, Tyler, let's see if *Alf* is on yet.

STAFF: *(Rolling back to block the door.)* That's really your fear, isn't it.

MARY: No, for your information, it's not. The discussion is closed.

(Unable to get to the door, she storms over to the empty basket, carries

it to the clothesline. Dry or not, she starts yanking clothes down and folding them with a fury.)

STAFF: She walked out of here and all you could see was her out in the back seat with some yahoo farmboy.

MARY: You stop this right now.

STAFF: You know it's true. You'd like to be worried about something worthwhile like her physical safety or state of mind. But when you get right down to it, your big concern is what she's out there doing with her private parts! You might as well just admit it.

MARY: *(Stuffing clothes in the basket.)* That isn't all I'm worried about, Staff.

STAFF: The hell it isn't. What was your mental image when she left here?

MARY: My what?

STAFF: Your mental image. What were you picturing?

MARY: Staff, now quit, I mean it.

STAFF: You were picturing her going at it with some kid, weren't you.

MARY: You're being stupid now.

STAFF: You were. You know you were.

MARY: You think that isn't tied up with the rest of it? You think she'll be happy if she gets pregnant? You think she won't be lonely if none of her friends have anything to do with her? You worry about one thing and you're worrying about the rest. It works that way, Staff.

STAFF: How far'd you take it?

MARY: Take what?

STAFF: This night of unbridled lust. You've already got her a pregnant outcast, how much farther did you go?

MARY: That's not…

STAFF: Did she die? Some back alley abortion kill her, did it?

MARY: Stop it now! I mean it, Staff!

STAFF: And of course that's not all the farther we can take it, is it. Oh, no, not even death can stop our worries. We've got the everlasting soul to think about—

MARY: *(Almost a scream.)* Stop it!

(This outburst seems to shake Staff. Or maybe satisfy him. He sits and looks at her. She holds his gaze a moment, then picks up the basket of clothes. She marches onto the porch and stands silently waiting for him to move away from the door. He wisely does. She goes on through, the screen door closing behind her. There's a long silence.)

STAFF: *(Softly.)* There's nothing you can do about it, you know. Either way. That's all I'm saying.

(Another long silence from inside. Finally—)

MARY: *(Offstage.)* Maybe.

STAFF: Like the rain.

MARY: *(Offstage.)* Maybe.

STAFF: Just think about it.

MARY: *(Offstage, more pain than anger.)* There's more than one way to make a point, though.

STAFF: I guess.

MARY: *(Offstage.)* There's a kind way and an unkind way.

STAFF: I always seem to do it the unkind way.

MARY: *(Offstage.)* Any more you do.

STAFF: Didn't I always?

(There's no answer from inside. Then we see her face through the screen door, looking at him sadly.)

MARY: No.

(The truth of this hits him.)

STAFF: *(Quietly.)* Sorry. I've gotten old and mean.

(She steps slowly out onto the porch.)

MARY: You're not old. *(Staff laughs.)* What's funny?

STAFF: Nothing.

MARY: What did I say?

STAFF: It's what you didn't say. *(He sighs.)* I'm mean. I'm a mean man, Mary. That's a horrifying thing to realize about yourself. I don't think I set out to get mean.

MARY: It's okay.

STAFF: No, it's not. None of it's okay. I got old and mean. And then I got crippled. None of it is okay.

MARY: Honey, the doctor said it's just going to take time.

STAFF: I know what they said.

MARY: It's a loss, just like a loved one.

STAFF: I know. I've got to mourn my legs. I know.

MARY: There's stages.

STAFF: Don't tell me things I already know, Mary.

MARY: You're probably in the anger stage.

STAFF: I goddamn *know* I'm in the anger stage, all right? Don't goddamn *tell* me I'm in the anger stage!!

MARY: *(Indicating Tyler.)* Staff…

STAFF: Goddammit, Mary, he doesn't know what I'm saying!

MARY: He does too, Staff! He does!

STAFF: He does not! He just sits there and grins! I could tell him I'm gonna blow my goddamn head off and he'd never bat an eye!

MARY: Staff!

STAFF: No! I'm not gonna do this anymore! It was bad enough when I could walk away. Now I can't even walk away. I can't go out in the fields and think my own goddamn thoughts anymore. So don't expect me to do it! *(He wheels around and rolls his chair over to Tyler.)* You understand that, do you, Tyler?

MARY: *(Almost crying.)* Staff...!

STAFF: You know what that means? I'm *here,* baby, just like you are. And your mama gets to take care of the both of us.

MARY: Staff, please...

STAFF: I'm no different from you now except I shit in a bag and you shit in your pants! *(Mary is silent now, standing in the middle of the porch. Staff seems to have run through some of his anger. He sits in front of Tyler, breathing heavily. Tyler just smiles his beautiful smile at him.)* And I am what I am, so you're both just gonna have to get used to it. *(There is a long standoff. Mary is frozen in place, Staff stares at Tyler. And Tyler just keeps smiling sweetly at his dad. Finally, still looking at Tyler, Staff speaks.)* Can you do that, Mary? Can you let me be myself around him? If not, you better let me know now. *(Mary is silent.)* I'm not just talking. I have to know now.

MARY: Can't you just be...

STAFF: *(Roaring.)* Now, goddammit!! *(There is a long silence. Staff speaks with a deadly seriousness.)* I can't act like there's something there, Mary. I can't watch everything I think and do and say as if there's someone in there.

MARY: But he *is* there, Staff.

STAFF: Because he laughs? He's there because he laughs?

MARY: Because he *loves,* Staff. He loves us, you can tell that.

STAFF: Is that life? Is it really that simple? 'Cause I thought mine out. All of it. My whole life. One the way off the barn roof. You know they say your life flashes before you? Well, it doesn't flash. It takes as long the second time as it does the first. But it's all there, like some long boring home movie that someone's making you sit through. And you keep saying to yourself, why the hell did I do that? I mean, every decision you ever made is right there and you're saying, why the hell did I do that? And the thing that's scary is that you can't do anything to change it. All you can do is watch. And you start to wonder if it's that way the first time around too. Anyway, I figured as soon as I'd watched the whole thing it'd be over, you know? I'd see myself climb up on the barn, drop the hammer, reach for it like an asshole, start to slide, say to myself, why the hell did I do that, and then I'd hit the ground. But it didn't happen. I went through everything in my life and I was still falling. Hours, it seemed. I figured I'd probably lost track of time, you know, but the longer I fell the more I started thinking—maybe I don't have to hit at all. If I haven't hit yet, maybe it's because of something I'm doing. And this thought went through my mind. It said, "I think, therefore I am." And I couldn't remember where I'd heard that before, but at that point I didn't give a shit where I'd heard it—I thought that was the key. As long as I was thinking, I wasn't going to hit the ground and stop being. So I thought my brains out. I ran through batting averages, tried to list every car I ever owned, named damn near every kid in my sixth grade class. Then I started thinking about you. Hell, just trying to figure you out kept me afloat longer than anything else. I came to two decisions about you on my way off that barn. One, you're probably the best person I've ever known in my life. And two, you're doing it all just because you think you're supposed to. That's why you didn't leave me a long time ago when you should have, because somewhere in the Bible it says you're not supposed to. It's why you would never put Ty in a home. And it's why you took care of my mom for twelve years. That woman never had a kind word to say to you, but you let her live in your house for twelve goddamn years. And you know why? Because that's what God would want you to do. *(Slowly.)* And that…got me thinking about God. That was my big mistake. Because as soon as I got to thinking about God I thought, hey, now might be a pretty good time to pray. I hadn't prayed in twenty or thirty years, you know, but as far as I could remember, it was a lot like thinking. So I thought, okay, I'll just pray for awhile here. But then, just like always happened to me even back when I was little—I couldn't think of anything to pray about. There's that little moment when you wonder what the hell you're doing. Are you talking to yourself? Or are you really talking to some being up there somewhere who created you and knows everything you think and do? And it that's the case, what do you have to say that he doesn't already know? And if you're gonna pray for something, like to not die, are you trying to get him to change his mind? I mean, did he already decide you were going to die, but you ask him not to let you die, so he goes, "Oh…okay." You start wondering this shit, at least I do. And I always did, you know? So just like before, I hit that point where I kind of blank out about what it was I was gonna pray about. You know, your mind just kind of goes blank for a second. And that was all it took. Next thing I know, I'm looking at a hospital ceiling.

(There is a long, stunned silence from Mary. She's never heard this much from Staff and it takes awhile to digest. Tyler gives a little chuckle.)

MARY: *(To Tyler.)* I love you, baby. *(She ponders awhile longer.)* Are you saying God let you hit the ground?

STAFF: *(A sad laugh.)* He sure didn't stop me, Mary, but that's not what I'm saying.

MARY: What are you saying?

STAFF: *(Quietly.)* Jesus…

MARY: Staff, I'm trying to understand. Really.

STAFF: *(A strange urgency.)* My thinking kept me afloat, Mary, that's what I'm saying. *My thinking.*

MARY: Do you really believe that?

STAFF: I have to!

MARY: But you fell off the barn. You had to hit the ground sometime.

STAFF: But I didn't! Don't you see that? I was up there forever, all on my own! I was never gonna hit!

MARY: Honey, it just seemed like forever.

STAFF: *(Almost in tears.)* Don't say that! Don't you say that!!

MARY: But, Staff… *(They simultaneously look up. We hear the sound of a car driving in and stopping.)* Who in the world…

(Staff is quickly wiping at the tears in his eyes.)

TAMMY: *(Offstage.)* Hi!

MARY: Well, hi, Tammy! Come on up! Staff, it's Tammy and Brenda!

STAFF: I'm crippled, Mary, not blind.

(Tammy, a girl of seventeen, walks hesitantly onto the porch. Staff's imagery was correct, there is something of the mouse about her, but there is also a touch of condescension in her tone, as if she's speaking to children. She stops and gestures for her friend to come up too, but has

no luck. She makes an exasperated face toward the offstage car, then turns smiling to Mary and Staff.)

TAMMY: Hi, Mrs. Holcomb. How are you?

MARY: I'm fine, Tammy, how are you?

TAMMY: Just fine, just fine. Hi, Mr. Holcomb. I'm sure sorry… about… you know.

STAFF: Yeah. I'm pretty sorry, too.

TAMMY: You've been in our prayers at church. The youth group, too.

STAFF: Well, that's real nice of you.

TAMMY: I like to think God has a plan for everything. I know it's hard to believe that sometimes.

STAFF: Sometimes, yeah.

TAMMY: Like this drought thing. I think it's selfish of us to pray for it to end. That may be what we want, but God knows what he's doing.

STAFF: Is your father a farmer, Tammy?

TAMMY: No, a banker.

STAFF: Uh-huh.

(There is an awkward pause. Tammy turns her attention to Tyler, going right to him, patting his hand and speaking to him as she would a baby.)

TAMMY: Hi, Ty! And how are you? My, but you are getting so big these days! And handsome! Is that sister of yours here?

MARY: No, you missed her, Tammy.

TAMMY: Oh. Do you know where she went?

MARY: *(Slight pause.)* I don't think she said. You and Brenda want to wait? I've got some Cokes.

TAMMY: Um, no. Brenda's in kind of a hurry. We just wanted to say hi.

MARY: She'll be sorry she missed you.

TAMMY: *(After a moment.)* Did she go to the mall, do you know?

MARY: I really don't know, Tammy. She's going to stop for slushies on the way home. You might catch her at the Dairy Dog.

TAMMY: Oh, that's okay. We'll see her at school. *(She stands there a moment, fidgeting.)*

MARY: Do you want me to tell her you stopped by?

TAMMY: Oh…you could. I just wanted to show her something…! *(With a squeal, she holds up her left hand. On it is a ring with a small diamond.)*

MARY: Tammy Johnson—is that what I think it is?

TAMMY: Uh-huh! Michael down at church. He asked me yesterday.

MARY: Well, what a surprise!

TAMMY: He's going on his mission and didn't want to go without me. Two whole years, maybe more.

STAFF: You're marrying a preacher?

(Mary hides a smile.)

TAMMY: He's not a preacher yet. He wants to do some missionary work first. He says I can be a big help.

MARY: Where are you going?

TAMMY: We don't know yet. He says he wants to go where people need him most. There are countries where they still kill people for believing in Jesus. He wants to go someplace like that.

MARY: Well...that sounds kind of dangerous, Tammy.

TAMMY: Oh, I know. But can you imagine how rewarding it would be to save souls in a place like that? People would be laying their life on the line, just to believe in the Lord. They're hungry for it, Michael says.

MARY: I'm sure they are.

TAMMY: They believe in the strangest gods, some of them. The moon, the sun, giants they think live in the mountains or the jungle. Or, you know, Buddha or Mohammed or somebody. Michael says some of them might even think we're gods when they first see us. *(She giggles.)* Can you imagine that?

MARY: It's a different world over there, I guess.

TAMMY: But Michael says the killing is usually political. As long as they believe in these different gods, they can be controlled by the people in power. But wherever Jesus goes, democracy is right behind. So the people in power try to kill anyone who converts. It's pretty complicated, really.

MARY: Sounds it.

TAMMY: Well, I guess I better go, Brenda's in kind of a hurry. Maybe I'll stop over at Milo's house and see if Lindy's still there. I can't wait to tell her.

MARY: Milo?

TAMMY: Oh...didn't you...I thought you knew.

MARY: Knew what?

TAMMY: That she's kind of seeing Milo. I'm sorry, I thought you knew. *(She rolls her eyes.)* Oh, boy, is she gonna be mad at me.

MARY: Who's Milo?

TAMMY: Oh, just one of the construction guys on the new wing of the high school. I figured she told you.

MARY: No, she didn't.

TAMMY: Well, don't worry about it, it won't last. He's way too old for her. Boy, if she knows I slipped and told, she'll never speak to me again.

MARY: Well, just how old is this Milo?

TAMMY: Oh, he's—

STAFF: Is she over there now? *(There is a gravity to his tone that chills the women. Tammy suddenly isn't sure what to say or do.)* Little girl, I asked you a question. Is Lindy over there now?

TAMMY: I, um...I think so. She was, anyway.

STAFF: How do you know?

TAMMY: Well, I kind of saw your car there. I thought it was yours, anyway. It might not have been.

STAFF: So you knew she was there when you got here. *(Tammy is silent. Staff lowers his head for a few moments. The only sign of his rage is a clenched fist. Then the fist relaxes and he looks up, a touch of a smile on his face.)* You're a good girl, Tammy.

TAMMY: *(Relieved.)* Thank you. Well, I guess I...

(But before she can escape, Staff speaks up pleasantly.)

STAFF: You know, there's something I'm curious about. Maybe you can help me with it. *(Staff rolls over to the glider, picks up Mary's knitting and puts it in his lap. Then he pats the glider for Tammy to sit. She reluctantly does. Looks to him with not a little fear. But he reassures her with a smile.)* These...these people you're wanting to save— over there in the jungle or wherever—what are you gonna tell them when somebody comes into their village and starts chopping heads off?

TAMMY: *(Taken aback.)* What?

STAFF: Well, given that you're still there, you know, and not back in the States already, what are you gonna tell them when the troops come in and start killing everybody?

TAMMY: Well, whether that will really happen...

STAFF: But I thought that's what you said.

TAMMY: Well, I know it happens, but...

STAFF: Say it happens. What are you going to tell them?

TAMMY: I guess...you know, that there's a better place waiting for them.

STAFF: Where's that?

TAMMY: You know, heaven.

STAFF: You believe that?

TAMMY: Well, sure.

STAFF: All the way to your toes?

TAMMY: Well, sure.

STAFF: Enough to have someone die for it?

TAMMY: Well…*(Smaller voice.)* sure.

(Staff picks up the loop of yarn, leaving the ball in his lap. He starts to leisurely toy with the loop Tammy watches him carefully.)

STAFF: And because they believe in Jesus they'll get to go there.

TAMMY: Right.

STAFF: And what if you hadn't come along and told them about Jesus?

TAMMY: Um…I don't know. I guess they wouldn't go. I don't know.

STAFF: You don't know? You're gonna have people die and you don't know?

TAMMY: *(After a pause.)* Are you mad at me?

STAFF: No, I'm just a little confused about this stuff. Now, if they didn't know about Jesus in the first place…?

TAMMY: Well, I mean, if they'd never *heard* of Him…that's a different thing, I guess. But if I'd already *told* them and they still didn't believe…

STAFF: What then?

TAMMY: I guess they for sure wouldn't go. I think that's how it works.

STAFF: You think.

TAMMY: Yeah. Michael knows all that stuff better than I do.

STAFF: *(Still playing with the yarn.)* If they don't go to heaven, what happens?

TAMMY: You mean if they die?

STAFF: Right. If the troops come in and kill them.

TAMMY: Well, if the troops kill them for believing in Jesus, they'll go to heaven. I mean, that's why they kill them, for believing in Jesus. And they'll go to heaven.

STAFF: And what if they get scared of the troops and say they don't believe in Jesus?

TAMMY: You mean if they really do and just say they don't?

STAFF: Yeah. What if they decide heaven isn't worth getting their head chopped off?

TAMMY: Oh, but it is.

STAFF: Well, you and I both know that, but what about them? Say they realize they never got their heads chopped off for believing in the giant in the jungle. Say they decide it's a lot safer just to believe in him. Then what happens?

TAMMY: I guess they won't go to heaven.

STAFF: Where will they go?

TAMMY: Hell, I guess.

STAFF: You guess?

TAMMY: Well, yeah, they'd go to hell.

STAFF: That's what you'd tell them?

TAMMY: Well, Michael would. I'd just agree with him.

STAFF: So getting their heads chopped off would be better than going to hell?

TAMMY: Well…sure.

STAFF: Why?

TAMMY: Cuz…hell goes on forever.

STAFF: And the head chopping would be over with real quick.

TAMMY: Right.

STAFF: So a quick head chop is a lot better than an eternity in hell.

TAMMY: Right.

STAFF: Okay, it's starting to make sense to me. So hell must be a pretty bad place to be, right?

TAMMY: Well, sure, it's the worst place.

STAFF: What makes it so bad?

TAMMY: *(A smile to Mary.)* Come on…

STAFF: Hey, I haven't been to church for years, Tammy, you know that. And I almost died falling off the barn. I should probably know these things, don't you think? What makes hell so bad?

TAMMY: Well, I guess it hurts a lot. Jesus said it's like a lake of fire and you tear your hair and gnash your teeth. I guess it hurts a lot.

STAFF: Hurts so much you tear your hair out.

TAMMY: Right.

STAFF: And you stay there forever.

TAMMY: Forever and ever.

STAFF: So once you piss God off, he stays pissed off, huh? *(Tammy looks to Mary. Mary just smiles at her and shrugs.)* I mean, that's it, right? You had your chance and you blew it and the big guy is just gonna toss you down there to fry for the rest of eternity.

TAMMY: Mrs. Holcomb…

MARY: You're on your own, sweetie.

STAFF: So you're not really trying to save souls *for* God as much as you're trying to save souls *from* him.

TAMMY: No! That isn't it! God is Love. He loves us. He sent Jesus down to die for us so we wouldn't have to go to Hell. He loves us that much.

STAFF: Loves us so much that if we blow it we live in agony for the rest of eternity?

TAMMY: But that's why we have free will. We can choose to do the right things.

(Staff nods as if satisfied. Then he casually holds the loop of yarn out toward her. Uncertain, but dutiful, she lets him stretch the loop between her hands. Then he starts winding the yarn from her hands to the ball, talking quietly the whole time.)

STAFF: I had a dog I loved once. Still have him as a matter of fact. But, you know, much as I loved him he kept doing bad things. And he knew better. You could tell he knew because when he'd do something bad, like chew up the carpet, he'd always hang his head when you came in the door. You'd know he'd done something bad and you'd just have to go find out what it was. So I knew he knew it was bad. And that's what pissed me off more than anything. I mean, if he didn't know any different, you could kind of give him a break. But he *knew.* So one time I had just had it with him. I took him to the basement and tied him to the workbench and started torturing him. You should have heard him scream, it was awful. I was gonna just kill him, but I figured that was too good for him, you know, he might not learn his lesson. So I just keep him down there, torturing him. He's still there, the poor son of a bitch. Give him enough food and water to keep him alive. Go down there whenever I feel up to it and torture him some more. I mean, I have better things to do with my time than torture that dog day and night, but I have to, you know? *(Tammy is silent, stunned.)* Right, Tammy? I mean, you understand. He kept doing bad things.

(She tries to delicately disengage her hands from the loop of yarn.)

TAMMY: I should go. Brenda's in kind of a—

STAFF: But you know, I'm starting to have second thoughts now. *(She can't get away. He just keeps winding the yarn from her hands to the ball.)* I mean, just how bad was that dog? Does he really deserve what I'm doing to him? Help me out on this, would you? Just how bad does that dog have to be to deserve this endless torture? Lay out some ground rules for me.

TAMMY: I really should go now…

STAFF: Okay, he chewed the carpet up. It pissed me off, but was that really enough to deserve what he's getting?

TAMMY: I…um…

STAFF: *(Faster and faster with the yarn.)* And he pissed on my little pine tree so much it died. Now he knew better, you see, but he kept pissing there anyway.. You think that was enough?

TAMMY: I don't know.

STAFF: *(Almost angry now.)* And he bit the mailman all the time. I told him he couldn't bite the goddamn mailman and get away with it, but would he listen? Hell no, not that dog.

TAMMY: I really have to go, Brenda's…

STAFF: But you know what the last straw was? He wouldn't believe in Tyler, can you imagine that? Now, true, he'd never seen Tyler, but what does that have to do with it? If I say he has to believe in Tyler, goddammit, he has to believe in Tyler! You see what I'm saying here, Tammy? I mean, there has to be a line he's not allowed to cross, otherwise, what's the point of this life, right? I mean, if there isn't a basement you can send people to, no telling what they'll do, right? Right??

TAMMY: I…I really don't know.

STAFF: *(Throwing the yarn to the ground.)* So you tell those people in the jungle about me and my basement! If you can't scare 'em bad enough about God and Hell, you tell 'em about me and my basement!

TAMMY: *(After a long, horrified moment.)* You're mad at me, aren't you? *(To Mary.)* He's mad at me, isn't he?

MARY: I'd say so.

TAMMY: *(quavering)* But why?

MARY: For a number of reasons, honey.

STAFF: *(Pounding his hand.)* For making things so goddamned ugly!

TAMMY: *(Starting to cry.)* But I didn't…

MARY: *(Very calm.)* Let her go, Staff.

STAFF: *(Rising in pitch.)* For taking God and making him into a psychopath and dragging him into the jungle!

MARY: Let her go, Staff.

STAFF: *(Voice cracking in rage.)* For standing in judgment of my daughter and expecting me to do the same!

MARY: I love you, baby.

STAFF: *(A cry from the earth.)* For praying for souls instead of rain!!!

MARY: *(Very calm.)* I love you, baby. You hear me? I love you.
(There is no sound but a wrenching sob from Staff. Both women are still, Tammy from horror, Mary from concern.)

STAFF: Oh, god, I pulled my bag loose. I got shit running down my side. *(Tammy scampers around Staff's chair and off.)* Jesus god, I got shit all over me.

MARY: *(Going to him.)* We'll clean it up, honey. You and me, we'll clean it up.

STAFF: *(A wail, pounding at his thighs.)* My legs are dead! God, Mary, my fucking legs are dead!

MARY: *(Catching his fists, holding them.)* I know, baby. I know. It's gonna be all right.

STAFF: I'm gonna hit the ground. I try to keep thinking but I'm gonna hit the ground anyway.

MARY: *(Kneeling beside him.)* I'm here.

STAFF: Because you're supposed to be.

MARY: Because I want to be.

STAFF: Because of God.

MARY: Because of love.

STAFF: I don't believe in anything enough to keep from hitting.

MARY: Believe in me, then. *(She sits on his lap, holding him tightly.)* Believe in me. *(He cries into her neck. She holds him as if she'll never let go. Tyler laughs. She looks up at him and puts a finger to her lips to quiet him. He laughs again. Mary speaks softly to him.)* I love you, baby. *(Tyler laughs again, but Mary clings tightly to Staff. He laughs once more. Staff lifts his head and looks over at him. The stage is in near total darkness. Tyler laughs one more time.)*

STAFF: I love you too, baby. I love you too.
(Lights Out.)

END OF PLAY

Smith and Kraus *Books For Actors*
THE MONOLOGUE SERIES
The Best Men's / Women's Stage Monologues of 1995
The Best Men's / Women's Stage Monologues of 1994
The Best Men's / Women's Stage Monologues of 1993
The Best Men's / Women's Stage Monologues of 1992
The Best Men's / Women's Stage Monologues of 1991
The Best Men's / Women's Stage Monologues of 1990
One Hundred Men's / Women's Stage Monologues from the 1980's
2 Minutes and Under: Original Character Monologues for Actors
Street Talk: Original Character Monologues for Actors
Uptown: Original Character Monologues for Actors
Ice Babies in Oz: Original Character Monologues for Actors
Monologues from Contemporary Literature: Volume I
Monologues from Classic Plays
100 Great Monologues from the Renaissance Theatre
100 Great Monologues from the Neo-Classical Theatre
100 Great Monologues from the 19th C. Romantic and Realistic Theatres

YOUNG ACTORS SERIES
Great Scenes and Monologues for Children
New Plays from A.C.T.'s Young Conservatory
Great Scenes for Young Actors from the Stage
Great Monologues for Young Actors
Multicultural Monologues for Young Actors
Multicultural Scenes for Young Actors

CONTEMPORARY PLAYWRIGHTS SERIES
Christopher Durang: 27 Short Plays
Horton Foote: 4 New Plays
A.R. Gurney: Nine Early Plays 1963-1971
Israel Horovitz Vol. I: 16 Short Plays
Israel Horovitz Vol. II: New England Blue, 6 Plays of Working-Class Life
Romulus Linney: 17 Short Plays
Jane Martin: Collected Plays 1980–1995
William Mastrosimone: Collected Plays
Terrence McNally: 15 Short Plays
Eric Overmyer: Collected Plays
Lanford Wilson: 21 Short Plays
Humana Festival '93: The Complete Plays
Humana Festival '94: The Complete Plays
Humana Festival '95: The Complete Plays
Women Playwrights: The Best Plays of 1992
Women Playwrights: The Best Plays of 1993
Women Playwrights: The Best Plays of 1994
EST Marathon '94: One-Act Plays
Act One Festival '94: One-Act Plays
Act One Festival '95: One-Act Plays
By the Sea, By the Sea, By the Beautiful Sea: *McNally, Pintauro, Wilson*

CAREER DEVELOPMENT SERIES
Taken to the Stage: an Autobiography by Mimi Kennedy
The Job Book: 100 Acting Jobs for Actors
The Job Book II: 100 Day Jobs for Actors
The Smith and Kraus Monologue Index
What to Give Your Agent for Christmas and 100 Other Tips for the Working Actor
The Camera Smart Actor
The Sanford Meisner Approach
Anne Bogart: Viewpoints
The Actor's Chekhov
Kiss and Tell: Restoration Scenes, Monologues, & History
Cold Readings: Some Do's and Don'ts for Actors at Auditions

If you require pre-publication information about upcoming Smith and Kraus books, you may receive our semi-annual catalogue, free of charge, by sending your name and address to *Smith and Kraus Catalogue, P.O. Box 127, One Main Street, Lyme, NH 03768. Or call us at (800) 895-4331, fax (603) 795-4427.*